CONTENTS

SO-AXI-749

CHARISMA—DOES YOUR CHILD HAVE WHAT IT TAKES?

"We find delight in the beauty and happiness of children that makes the heart too big for the body."
— Ralph Waldo Emerson

There are over 10,000 children in the United States working as child models, some making annual incomes well into the five-figure range. Their beautifully innocent, slightly mischievous, forever endearing faces capture the attention of millions in a wide spectrum of media. Every day we read newspapers and magazines. We look at billboards. We watch TV shows and commercials. Children are everywhere — selling, or spellbinding us with their charm and talent.

More children today than ever before are modeling and acting their way into the living rooms, shopping malls and theaters of America. Advertisers of fashion, products and services are planning more events and writing more scripts using children as their central theme. The awareness of children's vast appeal in the marketplace is ever-expanding.

While beautiful women and men may be intimidating to the general public, children are not. Have you ever seen a child on a TV commercial, on a box of diapers or in a fashion catalog that you didn't like?

The innocence of children stirs our hearts. Sometimes we are profoundly amazed at their ability to act and talk. We enjoy watching them express themselves in ways that only a child can.

Is your child one who will uniquely express himself to the world, or at least to a part of it?

The Ranks of Mini-Stardom

If you are considering launching your child into the exciting but competitive ranks of mini-stardom first ask yourself, does your child want to? It's an essential question to consider before taking a single step forward. Your child's desire to model or act will play a huge part in his potential success in the business.

If a child doesn't want to be a model, it shows. Reluctant kids lose that special sparkle and zip. Modeling requires an outgoing, friendly disposition and a lot of patience and perseverance. It is difficult for children to maintain the glow and enthusiasm needed if they'd rather be playing football or practicing ballet. You can force them to go to the set, to put on the clothes and to get in front of the camera, but you simply cannot force them to "turn on" when they are turned off.

Most babies will have a good disposition for modeling if they are generally happy and smiling gleefully at friends and acquaintances. Consider it a good sign if they don't cry or cling to mother when a stranger is around. Also the baby should be healthy, not colicky, or throwing up frequently. And, believe it or not, there are babies who do not slobber during the teething phase — these babies are much in demand.

If your child is older, don't just observe him or her. Talk to them about their interest in acting and modeling. Some kids constantly pipe their dream of being a fashion model. Others love to memorize TV commercials and are always impressing their families and friends with their own rendition of the newest TV spot. While this kind of behavior can often be a good indication of the child's inherent desire, you will actually need to pose the question this way: "Do you want to go into a studio where there are lights, cameras and lots of people? Would you mind changing clothes often and staying still for at least one or two minutes?" Emphasize to your children that they will have to do what the people on the set tell them.

If the child is over three years of age, the parent is usually required to stay in the reception area while the child is in a photography session. The child will generally be less self-conscious and better behaved if the parent isn't there watching him. Most parents will unconsciously be motivated to direct the child. This becomes distracting to the crew — art directors and photographers — as well as to the child. So you may want to explain that you won't be with him while he is actually modeling or acting.

Children need to understand as much about the business as they possibly can. You are the best one to help them visualize the type of work they would be doing. The child needs to understand he may have to miss

You can begin to assess your own child's aptitude and desire to be a professional model by observing certain personality traits:

❏ Is he outgoing?

❏ Does he like to be around people rather than shying away when approached by strangers?

❏ Is he generally well-behaved yet alert to what is happening around him?

❏ Does he listen attentively to you and respond to your direction?

These are some questions that will help you get closer to truly knowing whether your child has the desire and personality for the business.

is a compelling attractiveness, an inexplicable charm, a magnetism that makes you want to take a second look. It's that special something like adorable freckles, twinkling eyes or gorgeous hair. It combines the obvious quality of being cute or good-looking with the indefinable, elusive quality of a magnetic personality.

soccer practice, dance lessons, rehearsals and birthday parties occasionally when his schedule conflicts with his modeling assignments. This means in order to succeed kids need to make a commitment to their modeling/acting work. If they are still exhibiting enthusiasm after your talk, you've both made a good start toward your final destination — a modeling career.

Got That *Special* Look

A child's charisma is the initial attribute child modeling agents search for. But just what is charisma? Charisma is a compelling attractiveness, an inexplicable charm, a magnetism that makes you want to take a second look. It's that special something like adorable freckles, twinkling eyes or gorgeous hair. It combines the obvious quality of being cute or good-looking with the indefinable, elusive quality of a magnetic personality.

The needs of the advertiser or talent buyer actually dictate the type of looks that seem to sell in the marketplace, depending on the nature of the project. There are four categories of "looks" sought after by most talent buyers. Familiarity with these looks may make it easier to understand what kind of model or actor will work best in a particular modeling situation. Many kids fall into more than one category. With the skilled use of a comb or a change of clothes, for example, you can often alternate a child's looks between the fashion look and an all-American look. Let's take a look ourselves.

BOY OR GIRL NEXT DOOR LOOK:

Light brown or blonde hair, healthy, average looking kid but bright.

ALL-AMERICAN LOOK:

*Pretty,
handsome,
blonde hair,
blue eyes
(the Kennedy look).*

FASHION
LOOK:

Sleek,
wears clothes
impeccably,
a classic
or stylish
appearance.

CHARACTER LOOK:

Disheveled hair, highly expressive face with funny grin, lots of personality.

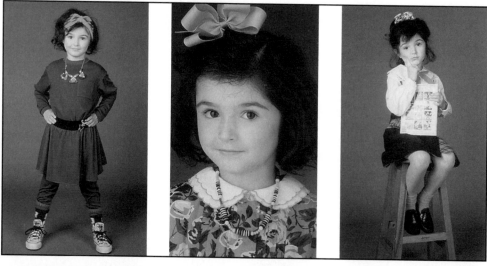

Beauty is in the eye of the beholder" certainly holds true in the modeling business. The beholder is the decision-maker who selects the child to model clothes or to represent a product or service. Generally, clothes retailers are looking for the child who fits the "fashion look"; those who want a child to sell a product or service will search for the child who best fits the "character look," "all American look" or "boy/girl next door look."

However, when it comes to selling a product there must be a balance between the child and the product. The seller wants a child who will enhance the product, not upstage it. This means that if the child takes center stage over the product, then the job of selling the product has not been done adequately. Directors and producers want a child who can act well in a mini-drama; a child who can play make-believe, yet remain believable without abandoning the reality of his true self.

An active imagination and intellect are tremendous assets for children who want to act in TV commercials. While a child who is atttractive will get his foot in the door on wit, it is his charisma, discipline, poise and a pleasing personality that will get him a step farther.

When the talent buyers or ultimate decision-makers screen children at an audition, they are searching for kids who exhibit character — who would look good holding their products or wearing their clothes — and who can talk best about their product or service. They are seeking that special sparkle or twinkle in the eye, maybe those cute freckles. Something that makes you want to take a second look, talk to them, kiss them, pick them up or pinch their cheeks. They may want someone who is energetic, yet not uncontrollable or wild. They are always looking for a child with special attractiveness and freshness and children with active imaginations. So the ultimate decision of who will be the chosen one rests within the eyes of the beholder — the advertiser.

The seller wants a child who will enhance the product, not upstage it.

Discipline Makes the Difference

Above and beyond everything else required to be a successful child model is one special quality — discipline. A child in this business will have to sit, stand and follow directions sometimes for hours on end. The minimum time requirement would be a one-hour booking. For a lot of kids one hour may seem like an eternity when they have to sit still and take direction on a set. Other children are willing and able to endure the long waits with humor, while viewing the process with fascination.

Kids frequently in a bad mood, clingers or spoiled kids will not be able to maintain their child-like professional stature. They may have the perfect look to get the job done, but if they are unable to endure the task with grace then the job will not get done.

An objective way of observing their aptitude is by frequently taking pictures of them yourself. Cajole them, ask them to smile, frown, appear intent or look thoughtful while you record these expressions on camera. Keep in mind though that while these are good at-home exercises for the child, the situation will be different at a studio in front of strangers. However, if you find they are responding to you and don't get too restless while you are working wih them, it is a very good indication that your child may just have what it takes.

They may have the perfect look to get the job done, but if they are unable to endure the task with grace then the job will not get done.

PROFILE OF A LITTLE STAR

*Damon
Giannatassio
"Character Look"*

Damon has a growing disorder. He was nine years old when he was selected through a talent search to be a star model. But he looked like a five-year-old.

In school he was constantly chided about his size. "Peewee," "pipsqueak," "squirt" and "shorty" were but a few names he was labeled. While short on size, he was tall on intelligence, good sportsmanship and possessed a maturity rare for his age.

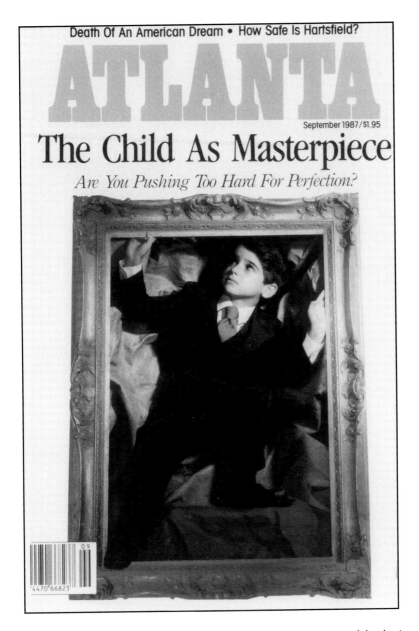

Death Of An American Dream • How Safe Is Hartsfield?

ATLANTA

September 1987/$1.95

The Child As Masterpiece

Are You Pushing Too Hard For Perfection?

Damon has appeared on the cover of ATLANTA Magazine, and has worked consistently for four years as a top department store model and TV commercial actor. His success brought him a new-found confidence and sense of self worth. His fame earned him the respect and envy of his fellow classmates. His size, which was once a constant sore spot, helped to make him one of the most sought-after models in the business.

Damon was selected from among 20 other nine-year-olds during an annual KIDDIN' AROUND MODELING AGENCY statewide children/young adult models search in Atlanta. He was unanimously chosen by an elite panel of judges because of his wonderful grin, his unique way of walking, his small stature and his absolutely bubbly personality. One of the judges on the panel had this to say about Damon: "There he was, at least five inches shorter than the other nine year olds. He was adorable because he looked so much younger, yet acted so much older. I personally felt that he could take on many different types of modeling jobs, particularly those requiring a boy around the age of five or six. I felt he could handle it with the maturity of a nine-year-old. He definitely strutted his stuff."

HOW TO LAUNCH YOUR CHILD'S MODELING CAREER

*"It should be noted that children at play are not playing about;
their games should be seen as their most serious-minded activity."*
— Montaigne

Unless someone approaches you or your child with an invitatition to model for a specific job, you will need to be the one to make the first move. We have all heard stories about being "discovered": You know, the one where you are walking down the street with your child and someone walks over and says, "Have you considered having your child star in a TV commercial? I may have a job for him." The next thing you know your child is starring in a TV commercial, and he's making more money than you could have imagined.

While this does really happen on occasion, most likely you will need to be the one to pursue the career for your child. Where do you begin? How does the modeling/talent business operate? Should you directly contact an advertiser such as Kodak, Coca-Cola, Macy's or the Hershey Corporation? The corporations who advertise are in the business of manufacturing, distributing and marketing their product or services. They do not have the inclination or the staff to handle and coordinate a child's modeling career. Instead they hire a modeling agency to do the work of securing talented children from whom they can then make a selection.

The child modeling agent functions as the liaison between your child and the advertiser. The agent is the professional who establishes a relationship with the various corporations with promises to provide them with the best models and talent in the business. It is their job to know what companies are producing print advertising or shooting TV commercials, and when and where.

The advertiser may call the agent on a Monday morning with this request: "We need two girls around the age of 9 or10, one white and one black. They need to be comfortable in front of the camera and able to deliver lines. They should be cheerful and very expressive. We'd like to see four candidates for each girl needed — preferably with some on-camera experience or training. The audition will be held on Wednesday at 2:00 p.m." The agent chooses from his talent all the children who meet those specifications and begins to call and book those available for the audition.

The Art of Selecting an Agent

PHOTO TIPS

Here are some tips for the types of photographs that will show your child off best.

❏ Make sure each photograph is clearly "in-focus" without shadows blocking the face or form.

❏ One photo should be a close-up of the child's face and one shoull be full-length.

❏ On the back of each photograph write your child's name, date of birth, current age, eye color, hair color, clothing sizes and a name, address and phone number where you can be reached.

The single most important goal is to find and establish a relationship with a legitimate and highly reputable client-active modeling/talent agency. You may want to consult the Better Business Bureau in your area for a listing of the most reputable agencies. However, one of the best ways to find out which agencies are the most popular is to call an art director or producer at a large advertising agency. Ask such professionals what agency they usually call for models and talent. Follow up that effort by asking friends and acquaintances for their first-hand recommendations. You should end up with two or three good agencies to contact.

The normal way to make your first contact with an agent is through the mail. You should send the agent two or three non-returnable snapshots of your child. It is not necessary to have these photographs professionally taken. The agents can tell enough from the snapshots you take at home.

It normally takes four to six weeks to get a reply from an agency. Most agencies only reply if they are interested in having you come in for an interview so they can meet you in person. Only a small percentage of children are invited for an interview. It is a good idea to send the photos to as many reputable agents as you can find. A particular agent may be looking for a certain type of look at that time and your child just may have it.

Finding a reputable agent is the primary objective. Just like in any business, there are "unprofessional types" who will try to lure you and your money into a shady deal. Your dreams can be built up by excessive superlatives, and then dashed to the ground by a large outlay of cash and no modeling jobs.

It is best to stay away from newspapers advertising for "Models Wanted." Legitimate modeling agencies receive numerous phone calls each day from people wanting to be registered with their agency. They do not have to advertise in a newspaper for models or actors.

A red flag should go up if someone wants to see you sight unseen. As stated before, most legitimate agencies will require seeing your child first from a photograph. It creates an embarrassing situation to have to tell a parent, face to face, that her child is too fat or doesn't have a marketable look.

Beware of those agencies who begin to pump you up right from the beginning. They know what you want to hear. Con artists and rip-off agencies will play off your vulnerabilty. They will have you believing that your child will be an instant success. You may be tempted to sign anything and pay any amount of money. They may even say you will be given a free training and photography session. If they are offering you several freebies, you can bet before it's all over you will end up paying for more than you get. Never sign a contract or lay out money on the initial visit with an agent. Sleep on it and make your decision after you've had time to think about it. A legitimate agency will never pressure you for an on-the-spot decision.

Remember, there are no guarantees in the modeling business. Beware if an agent says something like "Oh, you are just what we are looking for. We can guarantee you that you will be a star." Keep in mind, if it sounds too good to be true, in most cases, it will be. Always check with other parents who have children modeling for that agency before agreeing to work with them.

The normal way to make your first contact with an agent is through the mail. You should send the agent two or three non-returnable snapshots of your child. It is not necessary to have these photographs professionally taken. The agents can tell enough from the snapshots you take at home.

Getting Ready for the Interview

You've sent your child's photos to a reputable agency, and a month later the phone rings. Your child has been selected to come into the agency for an interview. Excitement mixed with anxiety overwhelms you. How do you dress your child and prepare him best for the upcoming appointment? Don't worry, because being and looking natural is what will work best.

Comb your child's hair the way your normally do every day. Don't tease it up or make ringlets. Of course, be sure the hair is freshly washed and brushed. Dress him in casual clothes. Put on his sneakers if that is what he usually wears. You want him to feel comfortable and relaxed. If you are anxious, most likely your child will be, too. It is best not to give your youngster any direction about how to act during the interview — except to be himself. If you instruct him how to act, his behavior may be the opposite of what the agent is looking for.

The following are some sample questions that may be asked of your child during the interview with the agent. Remember, you will be observed, too. The parent plays a key role in the child's modeling career. You are, in most cases, your child's secretary, accountant, chauffeur and personal assistant. You are the one who must take the directions for the modeling assignments and arrive there on time with everything needed for the shooting. Once on location, you will no doubt be expected to become "invisible." This means be prepared to take a back seat while your child is on stage.

We have interspersed questions directed at children of varying ages. Choose the ones most applicable for the age of your child.

Sample Questions for the Child	*Sample Questions for the Mother*
❑ How old are you?	❑ Do you work?
❑ Do you have a brother or sister?	❑ If so, how flexible is your schedule; how much notice do you need?
❑ What do you do for fun?	❑ How well do you know the city?
❑ What is your favorite toy, book, TV show, entertainer, thing to do?	❑ Do you have other children wanting to pursue a career?
❑ Do you have pets?	❑ If so, how will you handle one being accepted and successful, and the other not?
❑ Do you like having your picture taken?	❑ Are you willing to devote a lot of your time running your child around town for auditions?
❑ Do you pick up your toys?	❑ How much money can you afford to spend without a guaranteed return?
❑ When do you go to bed?	❑ Can you step back and let your child be directed by others without any input?
❑ What do you dream about?	❑ Do you have a reliable babysitter to care for your non-modeling children at a moment's notice?
❑ Do you ever get in trouble and why?	
❑ Why did you come to see me today?	
❑ Do you want to be a model?	
❑ What do models do?	
❑ Do you like changing clothes?	
❑ Do you like having your hair fixed?	
❑ Do you like school—what grades do you make?	
❑ Are you involved with any after-school activities?	
❑ Can you sing or dance?	
❑ What do you want to be when you grow up?	
❑ When you model you make money—what are you going to buy with the money?	

If the interview is going well, there are some questions you will want to ask the agent. Does she specialize in print advertising, fashion, TV commercials, feature films or all of the above? How many children does she represent? Will the agency show you some work their children have recently done? It's always a good idea to verify with the clients that the agent actually booked the child for the ad you are shown.

Your Place on the Map

Where you live in the United States will determine, to a large extent, the modeling opportunities available to you. Even though there is work to be found all over the country, the larger the market, the more work there is to go around.

The largest markets, New York and Los Angeles, are hubs of the advertising industry. Consequently, the percentage of working models and actors is greatest in those areas. Middle markets, such as Atlanta, Dallas, Miami and Chicago are areas where a large number of children are working. Even the smaller markets such as Denver, Minneapolis, San Francisco and Philadelphia enjoy a good share of the business.

If you live within a two-hour commute away from a major city, you can still be considered for modeling jobs in that area. If you live further than a two-hour drive to an active market, then you are "geographically unfortunate." There are simply too many models to choose from in the immediate area. It generally would not be worth a two-hour or more trip to go to an audition or a one-hour modeling assignment. Besides the fact that the child may get tired or cranky, if an agent needs you on short notice, it would in most cases be impossible for you to accept it.

For people living in smaller towns there are ways that you can still pursue a modeling career. The financial rewards usually are not great, but there are opportunities for children to model in shows and ads. If you have a mall or major department store in your area, call the mall special events coordinator, fashion coordinator or PR director. They will be able to let you know if there will be any fashion shows or modeling opportunities in their stores.

Many parents of would-be models and actors consider moving to a major market, such as New York, where the majority of the national work is booked. Parents who elect to move to New York do so at a great risk and an enormous expense. Even if the child has already been accepted by an agency, there are still no guarantees of the amount of work that might come from it. It is generally too risky a business for you to uproot your family to start all over — simply for your child's career.

If you already live in a major market or in commuting distance, then the opportunities will be more abundant. In New York, for example, many agents specialize in print work while others handle only TV commercials. These agencies require an exclusive agreement where your child works only with them. Many parents in New York hire a "manager" who works with different agents in securing jobs for the child. Managers also function as a booking agent for you. Generally, a manager is helpful if, one — your child is a busy, working model and two — you live in New York.

The smaller the market you live in the more prevalent "multi-listed" arrangements are — that is, working with more than one agency. It all depends upon the amount and type of work being done in that particular city. If the majority of work offered is done on a seasonal basis, then multi-listed work will be more common to that city than exclusive agreements. Also, in many cities such as Atlanta or Dallas, a single agency will handle the full range of print, television and feature film work done in that locale. You would then have a choice to be either multi-listed (work with more than one agency) or signed exclusively with one agency.

Many agencies sign on hundreds of children into their agency ranging in age from three months to eighteen years of age. While it may seem your child could get lost in the numbers, this is usually not the case. When you sign with an agency you form a partnership. For her services, an agent receives fifteen to twenty percent of the child's income. Obviously, agents want kids to audition and work as often as possible.

Even though the competition for signing on with an agent is great, the turnover of child models is even greater. There are a variety of reasons for this attrition rate. Children who are active modeling one year, don't want to the next. Families get transferred and leave the area. Children grow out of the popular sizes, lose teeth and become awkward. Children are constantly changing. This means that agents are always looking for bright, new talent to fill in the gaps created by these changes.

Once you are signed on with an agent, let her guide you to establishing the right hair, clothes and training for your child. An agent will know best what the advertisers are looking for, and what is in style. More importantly, the agent can help create for your child his or her own special "look" by working with the child's natural attributes.

FROM FASHION TO FEATURE FILM

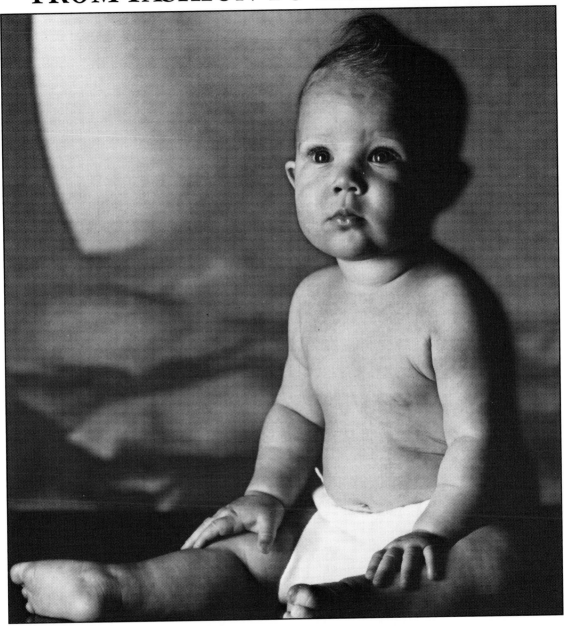

"Ah! What would the world be to us
If the children were no more?
We should dread the desert behind us
Worse than the dark before."

— Henry Wadsworth Longfellow

Advertising has as many different faces and expressions as there are children in the ads. In a relatively short time, the industry has skyrocketed into a multi-million dollar business. As a result, the number of Model and Talent Agencies around the country has swiftly multiplied, putting needed structure into the chaotic and complex world of advertising and motion pictures.

A modeling and talent agent is there to help educate and support you as well as secure work for your child. But it has become increasingly important for parents of prospective child talent to understand the full scope of the business. In this bustling and dynamic industry, the more you know, the more you will ultimately feel comfortable, communicate effectively and make intelligent decisions concerning your child's career.

The Many Faces of Advertising

There are two major areas of opportunity for models and talent in the advertising business:

❏ **PRINT**   ❏ **BROADCAST**

Within each of the major areas are several individual catergories that your child might work in. Print includes four specialized areas: FASHION print, PRODUCT print, COMMERCIAL print and EDITORIAL print.

When a child models for a print advertisement, it means his photograph will appear in ads placed in any of the following advertising media:

❏ newspapers   ❏ brochures
❏ catalogs   ❏ boxes, packages
❏ magazines   ❏ billboards

a **FASHION** *print kid*

You see fashion models selling all sorts of beautiful clothing, sparkling jewelry and attractive shoes. For most people, "fashion modeling" is the first area that springs to mind when one is considering a modeling career. The image of fashion holds glamour and appeal. A less well-known fact is that the fashion industry is actually one of the most competitive areas of modeling. It can be very lucrative and glamorous, but a child's fashion modeling career is short-lived and entails meeting a rather specific list of requirements.

The fashion model's job is to entice shoppers to buy. This is one area of modeling where surface "looks" are everything. The typical fashion model is well-proportioned with either an all-American look or an unusual exotic look. The cute "Opie" look usually won't make it. Most fashion catalogs and magazines feature children who are poised, graceful and really show off the latest fashions with impeccable style.

Besides having the "good-looking, beautiful" status, the child needs to fit into sample sizes. The truth is the bulk of fashion modeling goes to kids who wear the sample sizes of 2T-3T, 5-6, and 10-12. Infants have no particular sample sizes. They are either booked according to their weight in pounds, such as 0-10 pounds or 11-18 pounds, or according to their age in months, such as 9, 12, 18 or 24 months.

There is a good reason that most of the work is done in sample sizes. Designers usually are busy designing their new lines one to two years ahead of the selling. They make sample styles in three sizes (small, medium and large) so that the retailer/merchandiser can see how they look per size. When the merchandiser purchases a line of clothing, it then becomes necessary to prepare the advertising materials usually three to six months ahead of a season. The samples are used for the advertising photography session and the catalogs are produced so the consumer can view the clothing catalogs before a season.

The three busy fashion seasons for children are Easter, Back-to-School and Christmas. Parents and grandparents spend the most money on wardrobes for children on these occasions. The advertisers are busy producing nice, thick color catalogs a couple of months ahead of time. Consequently, these three annual occasions are the fashion model's "bread and butter."

Children who wear the off sizes of 4, 7-8, 14-16 and 18, are booked on occasion for fashion modeling. The retail stores have special sales during a season, such as Fourth of July, Labor Day and After-Christmas. They usually announce these sales through newspaper ads just prior to the upcoming sale. The client can pull from the in-store inventory to fit just about any size model.

A Fashion Print kid

a **PRODUCT** *print kid*

In product print modeling, it doesn't matter what size you wear or whether you have that certain fashionable look. As a matter of fact, it is more important to look relatively ordinary, so as not to upstage the product being sold.

Product print includes the entire spectrum of tangible goods sold in the marketplace. A child could model for ads selling potato chips, hot dogs, soft drinks, bicycles, skateboards, dolls, games, automobiles, TV sets or stereos. The list goes on and on as do the opportunities for product print modeling.

"Character look" models are selected more often to do a product print ad than any other. Ocassionally a fashion model can make the transition and be selected to appear in a product ad. But again, looks can distract from the product if the model is too pretty or handsome. The consumer's attention will be drawn to the model's face rather than the product. Keep in mind, the product is the star, the talent the prop.

The most important attribute child models can have is to be believable in whatever scenario they are asked to play — whether it be enjoying the best hamburger money has to buy, or having a great time playing with a Barbie doll. It could simply mean expressing excitement with the brand new Chevrolet Dad just brought home for mom. There are specific roles the child must play or situations he must make believe. Many kids can teach an adult a thing or two about the world of imagination.

With Our New Dictionary, She'll Enjoy Success Across The Board.

The Lincoln Writing Dictionary. HBJ can give every student a winning way with words.

We've combined the first all-new children's dictionary in a decade with an outstanding collection of writing resources, all in one volume. In addition to clearly worded definitions, we've included 600 articles designed to refine writing skills and 4,000 quotations from literature that demonstrate the best English usage. Our attractively readable format invites browsing, and the exciting visuals will also earn high scores. So, give your students *The Lincoln Writing Dictionary,* then watch them get ahead of the game.

HBJ Harcourt Brace Jovanovich
School Department

To order, call 1-800-CALL-HBJ. For more information, write A.L. Brooke, Harcourt Brace Jovanovich, School Department, Orlando, FL 32887.

A Product Print kid

America's kids are hopping, running, skipping, jumping, dancing, dashin

a **COMMERCIAL** *print kid*

Commercial print work encompasses all the intangible goods or services offered to the general public. Airlines, insurance companies, day-care centers, hospitals, learning centers and amusement parks are just a few examples. The service-related industry is booming, with more and more advertising dollars allocated each year. The opportunities are mushrooming for models because every service needs a person to demonstrate its need or desirability.

Say Disneyland is auditioning children for a magazine ad featuring its famous roller coaster. Since the ad is not a TV spot but rather a still photograph, the child might be required to hold an animated, excited expression while sitting in a roller coaster. Although the latest high speed film does enable a photographer to stop fast action, more controlled environments are generally needed.

A hospital might produce a print ad showing a sick child rushed to its first-rate emergency room. Here the child might need to wear special makeup and act as if in pain and discomfort. In this case, a child's imagination is utilized to the maximum, and his success is dependent upon his ability to be believable in the eyes of the camera.

ncing and singing to the music of Sandi Patti and the Friendship Company.

Product print kids in a billboard ad

Commercial print work encompasses all the intangible goods or services offered to the general public.

SPECIAL EDUCATION

A Struggle to Learn.

Everyday Amy struggles in school. Her handicap makes it hard to do what comes easy to others. How can special education make a difference? John Pruitt looks at the program for special kids in our schools and how early intervention may aid your child's struggle to learn.

Monday 11pm 🌻

11ALIVE NEWS *EXTRA*

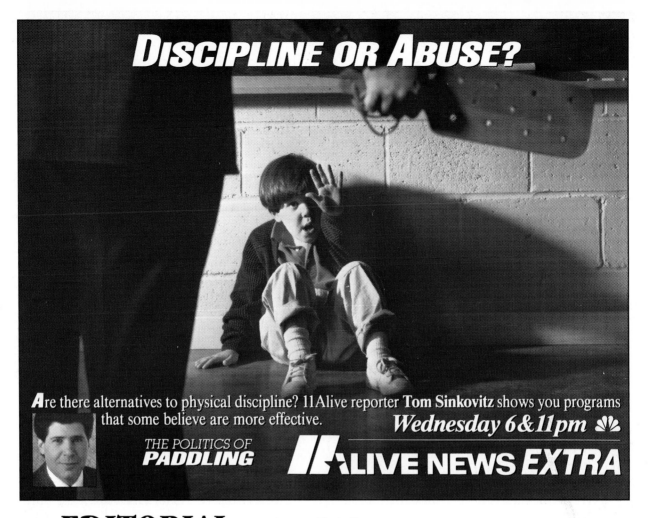

DISCIPLINE OR ABUSE?

Are there alternatives to physical discipline? 11Alive reporter **Tom Sinkovitz** shows you programs that some believe are more effective.

THE POLITICS OF **PADDLING**

Wednesday 6 & 11pm

11ALIVE NEWS EXTRA

an **EDITORIAL** *print kid*

This type of print differs from product and commercial print by being primarily an informational form of advertising. Although product and commercial print do inform the public, they are definitely selling a specific item or service to be purchased.

Fashion editors of newspapers and magazines use models to show upcoming fashion trends. The magazine *Vogue for Children*, for example, traditionally displays page after page of fashion ideas. One month *Vogue* may feature hats and gloves as making a comeback, and the next month a special issue on the newest look in pajamas. The publications are not selling a particular designer label, but rather informing parents and children of the latest fashion statements.

The food section of the newspaper may do a feature on some ideas of what children will be carrying in their lunch boxes during the upcoming year. The newspaper ad may show a few models on their way to school with a lunch box in hand full of goodies.

Sponsored, non-profit magazine and newspaper ads are frequently produced, educating and warning children about problems, such as the harmful effects of drinking while driving.

The sole purpose of editorial print advertising is to bring some type of information to the public's attention.

A whole series of ads has been done on the addictive nature of various drugs. There is an expanding need for "editorial print" models as our society continues to become more involved with the education and welfare of our country.

39

A Television Commercial kid

a TELEVISION COMMERCIAL *kid*

While many parents seem to enjoy seeing their child's picture in a print ad, TV commercials offer enormous potential for children wanting to work in the business. Most of the big money is made by children starring in national TV commercials (national refers to commercials aired in virtually every area in the United States). Advertisers pay TV commercial talent and film crews premium rates for their work. It's been said that five times more money is spent on TV commercials that air during a half-hour sitcom, than on the sitcom itself.

The "commercial kids" that are actively working are not the classic beauty types. Many have freckles or teeth missing. The most popular look for commercials falls in the "kid next door" category. The child you see sitting in the classroom, walking through a mall or riding the roller coaster at Six Flags has the type of "look" most advertising producers and directors generally choose to promote their products or services. This opens opportunity for a wide range of kids possessing many different looks and personalities.

Not only is there the advantage of a thousand different looks, many times there are several parts to play in any one commercial produced. For example, say McDonald's has a new TV spot concept. They want to show two girls and three boys singing and dancing about what satisfaction you get from eating a "Big Mac." They begin casting for a black girl with an upbeat, exceptional singing voice (around the age of 11). They need one other girl and three boys around the same age, who can sing and dance.

Also, the commercial calls for four other children who will sit in a booth at McDonald's, eating their Big Macs and rocking to the music. Here we have a total of nine children for one spot. Five of the kids will need specific singing and dancing skills, but the other four only need to act deliciously happy while eating their burgers.

There is no doubt that TV commercial acting is highly competitive, but two things are in play here. One, it opens its doors to a variety of looks and talents, and two, it provides opportunities, more times than you might expect, to inexperienced child actors. If a child can get a few TV commercials under his belt, it will help set the stage for a potential motion picture role.

a FEATURE FILM *kid*

All your child needs to make it in the film industry is a little TLC. Not the tender loving care kind of TLC, (although it always helps), but a combination of real TALENT, a good LOCATION and a lucky CHANCE. If your child has innate talent for acting then you have a good start. If you live in an area where movies or TV series are made, then you are doing better. If you have or intend to have a talent agent, then you have increased your chances and are on your way.

Many acting children made it to the ranks of stardom by taking voice and acting lessons and playing smaller roles. In the making of a movie, there are numerous "extras" used in various scenes, where the child may be seen sitting in a classroom or running in a playground. While these parts don't pay as well as the major character roles, they provide an excellent proving ground for future work. It does take an investment in time and effort to prepare the child for a film career.

Most of the TV series work is done in New York and Los Angeles. Living in or commuting distance from these two major cities is mandatory. However, motion picture films are shot around the country, although usually produced from a major city. When shooting "on location" versus at a motion picture studio like UNIVERSAL, producers will hire talent near the location in which they are filming. The South has become more popular as a location to make movies, and MGM, UNIVERSAL and WALT DISNEY STUDIO have recently opened in Orlando, Florida.

Landing a part in a movie or TV series can be a wonderful experience for a child, but it will consume his life for the time he is involved. Moviemaking sometimes takes six months, and often entails a 12-14 hour workday. Dedication, determination and patience are certainly cultivated in the children who work in film.

◆　◆　◆

The old cliché of being in the right place, at the right time, with the right person is certainly applicable to the modeling and talent business. But as in all successes, we find that if we possess the talent, energy and intelligence to pursue our dreams, we can usually make it happen. Perhaps your child can find his niche in the modeling and talent business— anywhere from fashion to feature films.

CHAPTER 4

TOOLS OF THE TRADE

"Children are the true connoisseurs.
What's precious to them has no price — only value."
— Bel Kaufman

As you know, getting signed on with an agent is the first step in kicking off your child's new career. Until the agent has issued an invitation to sign on, you really should not have invested any money, except for maybe a haircut or a new outfit of clothing. At the time of the interview, the agent should inform you, in detail, of the expenditures you might expect to incur if you decide to have him represent your child. After registering with an agent, you'll need to get a few things done. To get the wheels of your child's new career adventure spinning, he'll need to have a calling card made — that means photographs shot and printed. The agent may suggest some form of training either provided through the agency or a particular acting school. And, after your child's photos are made and he gets his first booking, you'll need to start packing a model's bag. Once he has completed his first assignment, you're on your way to building his portfolio. These are the "tools of the trade" that every model and talent needs to meet the open road — full steam ahead.

A Picture Is Worth a Thousand Words

In order for an agent to begin marketing your child, you will need to have professional photographs made. These are called headsheets, composite cards or test shots. The type of photography you need will depend on the area of advertising the agent decides your child is most suited for.

If you are invited to sign on by an agency that specializes in only print models or only TV commercial actors, then it has already been decided. If, on the other hand, you are invited to sign on with a full service agency that books models and actors in every area of advertising, they will inform you whether your child has the "fashion" look or the "character" look, and in which areas they feel your child can be most successful.

The 8 x 10 black and white **headshot** is the standard in the industry for showing TV commercial talent and movie and theater actors. The shot should be a very simple picture from the shoulders up. It should say "This is me. This is how I look." Don't be afraid to have your child try a few different expressions. One might be a pleasant smile and an another a serious, penetrating look.

It's generally a good idea to stay away from wearing black for your photo session. It tends to lend undue harshness to the picture. It's also best to avoid wearing white, which causes a washed-out appearance. Any other color shouldn't affect the photo adversely.

If your child wears eyeglasses, go ahead and plan on taking a few photos with him wearing them.

If the agent will be able to promote your child both in commercial acting and in print work, then it would be a good idea to have two smaller photos printed on the 8x10 sheet.

One would be the usual "shoulder to top of the head" shot. The other would be a "character" shot. This one should show your child more actively expressing himself. This could mean a shot of him eating a hamburger with ketchup dripping on his shirt. The expression on his face could say "Uh-oh — mom is going to kill me 'cause she's going to have to wash my shirt in Cheer to get this stain out." Look for the shot that will help a client get a clearer picture of how well your child can sell a product or service.

Here's a sample list of items it might be best to avoid when planning for the photo session

❏ busy prints
❏ flowers
❏ large barrettes
❏ stripes on shirt
  or blouse
❏ heavy jewelry
❏ sunglasses
❏ ruffles or bows
  around the neck

HEADSHEET				
AREA OF ADVERTISING	**TYPE**	**SIZE**	**PHOTOGRAPHY COST**	**PRINTING COST** (100 Minimum)
TV Commercials, movie and theater acting	Black& White	8" X 10"	Approx. range $75-$150	(One-Shot) Approx. $.75 per card
Print Work	Black& White		Approx. range $150-$175	(Two-Shot) Approx. $.85 per card

For fashion and print models, the **composite card** is most frequently used for representation. They can be one-or two-sided composite cards, shot in either black and white or color. The standard size is 6" x 8".

It will cost a little more to have a two-sided card printed, so you may want to start off with the one-sided version. The composite should include a head shot, and from one to four different fashion or character looks. If your child is going to be a fashion model it will be important to show his versatility. One shot may show a boy in a suit or a girl in a dainty dress. The next shot could show the child dressed in a sporting outfit, like tennis or hockey

clothes. Or perhaps dress them up for a Ralph Lauren or Esprit look. Different hair-styles are also a good way to show off potential. However, the style of clothing and hair shouldn't be too trendy. Fads are short-lived, and you probably want to use the same composite cards for as long as possible. Reshooting is costly so keep the look as "classic" as possible.

Character models who want to use a composite card for print work representation, can use the different shots as a means to display their versatility. They can be demonstrating products, tieing their shoes or just standing there, hands on hips, with an "I dare you" look. The possibilities are endless. What you want to come out of your photography session with are the most original, marketable and unforgettable shots you can get of your child. These photos are the most important tool of this trade. And, the photographer who shoots your child is instrumental in the process of capturing your child's greatest assets on film.

DESTINY FOSTER

Hair Brown / Eyes Green / DOB 6-3-78

Height _____ Weight _____ Sizes _10_

Kiddin' Around
Models and Talent
482 Armour Circle N.E.
Atlanta, Georgia 30324
(404) 872-8582

Printed by Custom Photo Art (205) 326-3314

C O M P O S I T E   C A R D S

AREA OF ADVERTISING	TYPE	SIZE	PHOTOGRAPHY COST	PRINTING COST (100 Minimum)
Fashion Model and Print Model	Black & White	6" x 8"	Approx. range $175-$225	(One-Shot) Approx. $.75 per card
Fashion Model and Print Model	Color	6" x 8"	Approx. range $175-$300	(Two-Shots) Approx. $1.00 per card Add $.10 per card for each additional

The possibilities are endless. What you want to come out of your photography session with are the most original, marketable and unforgettable shots you can get of your child. These photos are the most important tool of this trade.

Printing costs vary depending on where you live in the United States. Your agent will be able to direct you to a printer who offers you the good quality printing you need at the most competitive rates. Not all printers are good ones. You'll be defeating the purpose of having first-rate photography if you use a second-rate printer. Remember, you get what you pay for in most cases.

Selecting the Right Photographer

A client chooses the children he will audition based on the photos sent to him by the talent agent. Selecting the right photographer can mean the difference between a mediocre photograph and one that is so good, it immediately catches the client's eye for serious consideration.

Here's an important tip for making sure your child's image is captured to its fullest: choose a photographer who specializes in the same area of advertising in which your child will be promoted. Some of the specialty areas of photography are food, architecture, wild life, fashion, sport and product.

If your child has been classified as a fashion model, hire a fashion photographer — preferably one who shoots fashion catalogs. This type of photographer shoots models for fashion layouts regularly. When he looks through the camera at your child, he will be visualizing him in a layout for a magazine ad or a catalog.

The same applies to a prospective commercial actor or print model. A "character photographer" who shoots print advertising for a living will prove invaluable to the outcome of your child's performance in the studio. The photographer has the experience necessary to offer creative advice, and to assist your child in appearing as natural and relaxed as possible.

Another advantage of working with these specialized photographers is that they also work for potential clients. If they like your child's looks and personality, it's possible they could recommend him for a modeling job with one of their clients. It also gives the children a chance to see how it feels to be in a professional, modeling environment.

It is best to avoid photographers who just shoot portraits. Their rates are generally higher, and often they are not as successful in capturing that perfect fashion look or that expressive character look. Your agent should be able to guide you in the right direction.

Character models who want to use a composite card for print work representation, can use the different shots as a means to display their versatility. They can be demonstrating products, tieing their shoes or just standing there, hands on hips, with an "I dare you" look.

Although you want to use the same composite cards as long as possible, it is crucial to keep them updated as your child grows and changes.

Lessons for Acting

Besides having a composite card made, it may be advantageous to have your child enroll in a training class. Generally, it is best to wait until after you have found an agent to represent your child. Modeling schools have some value, but they sometimes teach the children to do stiff poses or robotic moves in front of the camera. The more natural your child appears in a shot, the better. We've all seen those fake smiles and postures, and they are not what clients want.

Modeling schools have been known to charge anywhere between $400 - $1200. The training an agent should direct you to will depend on what kind of modeling your youngster will be doing. If he will be acting, it will depend on what level of acting skills he needs. Fundamental acting, theatrical acting and method acting are a few of the different types of classes offered. These training classes should cost between $200 to $400.

Agents send their children to instructors who are usually former models, or actors and actresses actively working in the field. These instructors know what casting directors and advertising agencies are looking for, and they help your child develop the right skills. A good teacher is an invaluable asset for your child's future enjoyment as a model or talent, and for his gainful employment in the field. Check carefully the instructor's resume — it will ensure that your child in good hands.

When your youngster has been booked for a modeling assignment, it's time to start packing. Not for vacation (although it could be tempting) — but for a "shoot." Your agent will apprise you of the exact kind of shoot you have been booked — whether it is fashion or commercial — so you will know, ahead of time, the kind of clothes and shoes needed for the assignment. The client provides the clothes for a fashion shoot, but usually not the shoes. Commercial jobs, on the other hand, require the child to come outfitted according to their direction, unless otherwise instructed.

You may be asked to supply various props for the shoot, such as a pair of wire-rimmed glasses, sunglasses or a baseball cap. If you are not instructed to bring a specific outfit for the child to wear, avoid visible designer labels, like Izod or Polo, on the front or back of shirts or pants.

Make sure your young model has freshly washed hair and clean fingernails. Comb the child's hair the way it was styled for the headshot or composite card, unless specifically asked to do otherwise. And, prior to the shoot, try to avoid feeding your child any foods loaded with sugar. Studies have shown that children with high intakes of sugar are generally more hyperactive. Cutting back on sugar might also help diminish the dark circles under the eyes if they tend to have them. Good luck on the shoot, and don't forget — you have a new addition to your child's portfolio.

Here are some suggestions for packing your child's knapsack with a few very useful articles:

For the Girl

- ❏ Tennis shoes (white regular and high top)
- ❏ Dress shoes — black or white patent leather (Mary Jane shoe) for an Easter fashion shoot
- ❏ White turned down socks, knee socks, frilly socks, stockings
- ❏ Toothpaste and toothbrush
- ❏ Comb and brush
- ❏ Bobby pins, barrettes
- ❏ Concealer for dark circles or boo-boos
- ❏ Transculent powder if needed to cut down shiny face
- ❏ Clips and masking tape for on-the-spot alterations
- ❏ Anti-static device or spray
- ❏ Favorite toy or homework

For the Boy

- ❏ Tennis shoes (white regular and high top)
- ❏ Dress shoes — penny loafer, lace-up shoe
- ❏ Suspenders
- ❏ Navy, brown, black socks athletic socks (white)
- ❏ Assortment of belts
- ❏ Toothpaste and toothbrush
- ❏ Comb and brush
- ❏ Styling gel
- ❏ Concealer for dark circles or boo-boos
- ❏ Clips and masking tape for on-the-spot alterations
- ❏ Anti-static device or spray
- ❏ Favorite toy or homework

For the Mother

- ❏ Newspaper, magazine or book for reading while waiting during shooting session
- ❏ Treat for child as an after-the-job reward.

Building the Portfolio

The headshots and composite cards you have shot for your child are not his portfolio. You build a portfolio by keeping samples of his work. These samples are called "tear sheets." Tear sheets are ads cut out of the newspaper, magazine or brochure. It's a good idea to purchase a small 8" x 10" portfolio carrying case to store the tear sheets. The standard size used to be 11" x 14" but over the last five years the 8 x 10's have become more popular. Some people even prefer the "mini cases" which are 5" x 7". Your portfolio case can be purchased from an art supply store for about $35-45. Many agents supply their own cases with the agency's name on the book.

What's really important is what goes inside. You can start the portfolio by having a few of your child's best shots blown up. But, as soon as he has completed his first job, be sure to ask the client or art director for a copy of the ad, **before** you leave the studio. Many ads are shot in one location, but released in other parts of the country. If this is the case, a person at the studio can give you the name and address of the person to whom you should write to obtain a copy of the ad. It will be necessary for you to compose a letter requesting a copy. Here's a sample one to help you get started:

Dear _____,

My child was in Franklin Studio on February 1, shooting an ad for your Easter catalog— Job XYZ. Could you please send me as many copies of the ad as possible?

Since your ad will not be running in the city I reside in, I'd be most appreciative if you would respond to my request. Enclosed is a self-addressed, stamped envelope for your convenience. Thanking you in advance,

Ms. "Child Talent's" Mother

The time to get your hands on the "tear sheet" for your portfolio is when your child is actually in the studio. It's important to remember to ask while you are there because the samples of your child's work are the tools he needs to build a portfolio.

Clients are much more impressed by actual samples of your child's work than by photos you had professionally shot. They realize a photographer could shoot a hundred rolls of film before getting one good shot.

Now that you have become more familiar with the various tools your child will need for his new venture, it's time to find out what auditions are like, and to take a peek backstage.

For children who are commercial talent, a "video" is used as their portfolio. You hire a video production company to take the master TV commercial your child worked in, and dub or copy it onto your personal videotape. Each time your child works on another commercial, they add it to your personal tape, with the most recent commercial always being the first on tape for viewing.

THE BUSINESS BACKSTAGE

"The entry of a child into any situation changes the whole situation."
— Iris Murdoch

L ights, Camera, Action!" The people on a film set spring into action when a director shouts those cues. The words hint of glamour and intrigue. But, behind them is a network of professionals, team players working to make concepts on paper come alive on film.

The complexity of a "shoot" determines what members need to be hired and how many. Some TV commercial shoots require as many as 15 professional players. It may take a casting director, two producers, a director and an assistant director, a photographer with two assistants, two electricians, a makeup artist, a set designer with two builders and a production assistant just to get rolling.

A print shoot for a magazine ad may require a less elaborate set-up. In the print world, an idea for the ad or catalog is first sketched out by the art director. After the concept is developed, a photographer is consulted who specializes in the appropriate area. At the least, a print shoot requires an art director, a photographer with one assistant and a stylist to adequately get the job done.

It is helpful for the family to understand the different jobs of the professionals behind the scenes. If you become familiar with what the various jobs are and who does them, it will benefit your child and his performance. You will feel more confident and prepared to handle the different situations as they arise more intelligently.

The Casting Session

To prepare for a TV commercial audition you will need to know:

- ❏ the product or service the commercial is selling
- ❏ the character role your child is auditioning for
- ❏ any particular style of clothing required
- ❏ any special skill your child might need (like jumping rope)
- ❏ what lines, if any, your child will need to learn

And, don't forget to find out exactly when and where the audition will be held.

The casting director holds auditions or casting sessions for actors in TV commercials, films, motion pictures, theatricals and made-for-TV movies. For TV commercials, the casting director is generally hired by the producer who gives her the casting specifications, or "specs," of the job. Usually, the film director also meets with the casting director to go over the TV commercial script and storyboard (frame by frame drawings which depict the sequential action in the commercial).

The casting director calls the talent agent with the description of what type of child is needed for the commercial. The talent agent searches the files for the appropriate child who fits the age group, looks and experience. The agent sends the casting director the headshots of the talent that meet the specifications.

The casting director does a preliminary screening from the talent and calls the parent to set up an appointment to come in for the audition.

Once you understand the basics about what the commercial and character are about, you can explain it to your child. It is best not to get overly involved in directing or preparing him for the audition. You really don't know what the casting director will actually request the child to do until the time of the audition.

Annette Stilwell, who has cast commercials for clients such as Delta, Blueplate Mayonnaise, Anacin, CBS and NBC, gives some advice: "When we audition children for commercials and films, they simply need to act and look real. Some mothers try to direct the child without having any knowledge of what we are doing in the audition. The mother is prompting the child or even threatening the child. It is amazing and disturbing. Sometimes they bring a five-year-old in who, honest to goodness, has had hot rollers in her hair for four hours. I would rather see a five-year-old who had never seen a hot roller in her life."

Most commercials on the air feature children who are casually attired with normal hair styles. In your excitement to win the audition, don't change your youngster's hairstyle or dress him up for a party. The best way to get the young talent ready for the audition is to make sure his hair has been freshly washed and combed, and his hands, nails and clothes are free of dirt and food. Act calm and don't make too big a deal of his upcoming performance. A relaxed child in casual clothes is much more appealing than one who is tense and overly dressed.

Once you arrive at the audition, you will be required to wait in the reception area. "When it is the child's turn to go in to the audition," Stilwell says, "it is OK for the mom to walk the child back and meet the people. But once the production begins, that is their cue to go and wait in the reception area. Just stay in the wings. Be where the child feels secure that you are there. And don't ever try to direct the child at the same time the director is doing it."

If, after the audition, your agent doesn't call you, your child didn't get the job. Rejection can be tough on you and your child. The reason one child is chosen over another is not a personal one. The director and client must narrow it down to one or two children who are most similar to what they had in mind. It is always best to concentrate on the positive aspects of the experience. A child who is not right for one job may be perfect for another. There will be other opportunities.

For print work, the auditioning process involves fewer people and less time. The art director, photographer or an assistant contacts the talent agent with the age, size of clothing and type of look they need. Again the agent reviews her files for the appropriate kids to send to the "go-see."

The go-see is usually held at the photographer's studio. The photographer often takes a polaroid of the child and asks to see the portfolio. When he meets with the client, he will take the polaroid shots and probably the composite cards of the children he feels closely match the concept profile.

For both print modeling and TV commercial acting, the final decision of who gets the job does not belong to the director, photographer or casting director. The go-sees and auditions are a screening process where specific recommendations are made to the client. It is not unusual for the client who is advertising the product or service to request a second or third audition callback to see, in person, the talent who have been recommended.

A Scenario: *Your Kid on Camera*

Imagine this scenario. . . Your talent agent calls you to set up an audition for a 30-second TV commercial for children's aspirin. Your child meets with the casting director who is holding the auditions. The casting director explains that the commercial is about a child who is sick and has to stay in bed until he feels better. The instructions are for the child to snuggle reluctantly in bed, looking ill. Your child and four others go through the routine individually, while each performance is videotaped.

Two days later, your agent calls with the good news. Your child got the "booking" (the job). She sets it up for an 8:30 a.m. call the next day.

Meanwhile the production crew, hired by the producer, is busy transforming a studio with four concrete walls and a concrete floor into a child's adorable bedroom. Pictures of clowns adorn a freshly painted wall. A large four poster bed sits next to a nightstand and a baker's rack full of stuffed animals is cozily positioned in a corner of the studio.

Thirty lights hang from the studio rafters, designed to create a special warm, night-time effect. A boom microphone has been strategically placed and the camera is ready to roll.

When you arrive at the studio (on time, of course) you walk into a flurry of activity. Time is money and each minute can cost hundreds of dollars. When on a production clock, there is not much time for small talk.

The makeup artist grooms your child for the shoot while you bide your time patiently in the waiting room. Finally, they are ready for a run-through or rehearsal with the talent — your child. When the director is satisfied with the preview, he calls for a take — this time with the camera rolling.

The director gives his assistant the cue to begin. The AD (assistant director) takes your child to his appointed "mark" and announces "Quiet on the Set." The rumbling in the studio comes to a halt. Silence is imperative on the set whenever sound is being recorded.

The director takes over and cues the crew:

"Lights," he shouts. The electrical throws the switch, and thirty lights flash up. "Sound," he commands. The sound person activates the recording mechanism. When the equipment is running at the proper speed, he replies back to the director, "Speed."

"Camera," he directs. The cameraman looks into the camera and pulls the trigger. "Rolling," he asserts.

A production assistant takes the clapboard in front of of the camera, "Take One, Scene One — Mark," he says and moves away.

"Action," the director says to your child.

Several hours later, when the shots the director needs are "in the can" (filmed), he shouts to the glee of cast and crew, "That's a wrap," (the shoot is finished for the day).

Backstage professionals work as a team to help children succeed.

A PHOTOGRAPHER'S PERSPECTIVE

A good still photographer's job is to capture people, places or things on film. A photographer has to be technically proficient and able to bring light, drama and artistic composition to a photograph.

Ford Smith is a people and fashion photographer. He has shot for Coca-Cola International, Days Inn and Macy's, to name a few. His ads have appeared in magazines such as *Gentleman's Quarterly, Seventeen, Mademoiselle* and *Vogue.* Ford feels that in addition to a photographer's technical and artistic ability, he must be able to develop a special communication with the talent.

"A good people photographer has got to be someone who knows how to get the most out of his talent," explains Smith. "One who can communicate with them and direct them. I have to be honest, I don't enjoy shooting every single child. But I do enjoy the children who have been trained properly and who are professionals.

"It is hard to ask a one-year-old or a newborn to be a professional, but once kids start to get around two years old and up, they can follow directions, and then I find it very enjoyable. They do some very unusual and spontaneous things. They can be very entertaining.

"A little bit of discipline helps so they can stay in line, but it is also nice to have that surprise once in a while that you didn't expect. If you are ready for it, you can get that one-in-a-million picture."

Ford also spoke of the positive and negative ways parents can affect the overall performance of their young talent. "Parents can prepare the child physically and emotionally for the shoot. They should avoid a confrontation on the way to the photo shoot that might put the child in a bad mood.

"For children under the age of two, it is always helpful if the parent has developed some code words and expressions to use that will make their infant smile or perform certain actions on command. However, after the age of two or three, I have found the children really perform better without their parents around.

"In some respects, the modeling industry is more work for the parent than for the child. But if the parent is willing to devote the time and money necessary to a kid's career, it can offer many benefits.

"If I had a child who I thought enjoyed being in front of the camera and had some amusing expressions," said Ford, "I would certainly give him the opportunity to try it out. Any child who tries modeling for any length of time will become quite at ease with his friends. And, any endeavor he might follow after modeling would be enhanced by the confidence he has gained in himself from being in front of the camera."

AN ART DIRECTOR'S PERSPECTIVE

In the print world, the direct mail fashion catalogs, the newspaper inserts and the magazine ads are first concepted and designed by an art director. Brad Harrison has been a Macy's fashion art director for five years. He describes an art director in his profession, as the "mother" of an ad. "An art director has to fumble between administrative work and creative work," Brad explained.

"The clothes that we use for a fashion ad are sent to us by the vendor. The most popular sizes they send us are 2T-3T, 5-6, 8-10 and 12-14. If for some reason the size they send us is inaccurate, we may need a model who wears an off-size, but that does not happen very often.

"An art director has to follow through with the concept of the ad. This includes designing the ad, booking the models, hiring the photographer for the shoot and art-directing the hair and makeup. You doctor it, you see it through and then you pay for it. So you are almost the mother of the ad."

"The children we book to do the ads, first of all, need to wear the size clothing the vendor has sent us. Then they need to be hams. They are less intimidated with strange people, which is what we are to most children — strangers. The shy child, no matter how cute, is usually not going to be able to do a good job.

"A parent can help by taking a lot of pictures of their kids and taking the children around people where they will get used to seeing different faces all the time. The biggest ordeal is getting a child used to strangers. The best kid is going to be a natural, so forcing a kid into the business is not going to work.

"And then there are the kids who are too trained. You can tell that their parents have posed them in front of the mirror for days and days. I have actually had children who numbered their poses one through twelve. This is kind of bad because they lose their spontaneity. It becomes too forced, too posed. I think the modeling schools tend to give them the numbered poses, and it does actually reflect on their performance. 'Quality training' can be positive. The 'natural' kids know how to pose, they know how to laugh, they know how to move and not every movement is a forced pose.

You can tell if they have never had any training before. But, you can work with a child who is inexperienced, as long as they're willing to work with you.

"Children who are modeling should be doing it because it's fun, not because their parents are forcing them to do it. Also, parents can help to avoid an unpleasant situation for a child coming to a modeling shoot with a bunch of strange people by, again, exposing them more to strange or unfamiliar faces as much as possible. If they become comfortable, they will be able to get along with anyone and be personable — which is hard enough for adults to do."

A COMMERCIAL PRODUCER'S PERSPECTIVE

A film producer is at the heart of every TV commercial production. Initially, he meets with the advertiser or advertising agency, and draws up a cost estimate for the commercial. This estimate is based on the storyboard concepted by the creative team. A producer must have an intimate knowledge of every stage of production — how many crew members need to be hired and paid, what kind of set needs to be built, how many talent need to be cast and paid, what kind of equipment needs to be brought in for the shoot (like dollies, cranes, lights) and how much post-production (editing, special effects, music) will cost.

Lisa Donini spends a lot of time working with kids. She is a freelance on-line film producer. Some of her work includes Athlete's Foot, Kentucky Fried Chicken, KinderCare, Ponderosa, and Captain D's Seafood.

"Money is a big deal," says Donini. "If the clients ask for something after the job has been awarded, I have to negotiate with them how much it is going to cost. I have to protect the production company from losing a lot of money, once they have the job. We bid on a job from the storyboard, which can be vague. You can be dealing with a lot of money that can be misappropriated between the initial idea that the creative team had and what actually ends up on film."

A producer must have an intimate knowledge of every stage of production:

❏ How many crew members need to be hired and paid
❏ What kind of set needs to be built
❏ How many talent need to be cast and paid
❏ What kind of equipment needs to be brought in for the shoot
❏ How much post-production (editing, special effects, music) will cost.

The film producer usually hires the casting director to screen the talent for the director. After the talent has been booked for the actual production, it's important for the parent to be prepared for the upcoming shoot and to have a flexible schedule.

"Don't plan anything the day of the shoot other than the commercial," Donini warns. "Not only that day, but that night. The parent should make sure the child knows that he will have to wait a lot. Take some toys that they can play with, that aren't terribly distracting, and that they can't hurt themselves with or get too jacked up about.

"Parents need to ask the agent before they go on a shoot, who their contact person will be. All questions they have should be directed specifically to that contact person. But the parent needs to be sure and ask the agent what they need to be prepared to do.

"Children, many times, get tired. By the time they get in front of the camera, they feel like they have already worked their day. There may be 35 adults sitting in the studio saying, 'please bite the hamburger one more time' over and over again. It is understandable why children lose their steam after 20-plus takes of the same action."

The parent needs to know going into it, all of the variables, and be as flexible as possible. If you think about it, the idea of children as mini-professionals is an unusual one. They do change the nature of any situation they become involved in. The experienced professionals who work in the area of advertising and film have seen the best and the worst of child and parent behavior. Their insights into the do's and don't's have developed from the hours and days spent with hundreds of different kids.

On the top of the list of insights to success is that the child must desire to work in the business and enjoy it. Some of the most heart-wrenching stories are of children whose parents have tried to make them into something they were not. It causes extreme anxiety, despair and ultimate failure in the endeavor.

THE DOLLARS AND SENSE OF IT

"Why, a four-year-old child could understand this report.
Run out and find me a four-year-old child.
I can't make head or tail of it."
— Groucho Marx

Most young models and talent enjoy working in the business because it's fun — it's challenging — and it's a great outlet for expression. Many treat it as a sport, something they work hard to excel at and feel good about. The money they earn, for those who understand it, is more like icing on the cake. Translated into adult terms, these young professionals sometimes work very hard and long hours, and deserve the monetary compensation they receive.

The model and talent industry is made up of an intricate web of pay scales and unions. The parents or guardians of these young professionals have to function as the child's "business brain." They need their parents or guardians to know what the different pay rates are for the different kinds of work they do, to fill out the necessary paperwork and to put their money to good use. The parents need the talent agent to advise and direct them in these crucial areas.

Print Rates

POINT OF PURCHASE *(POP) means that a model's face, likeness or image is at a point where a consumer makes a purchase.*

Print models receive the same wages whether they work for K mart or Neiman Marcus. The rates escalate with experience as they do in any profession. Usually, after a model or talent has performed five or six jobs, the agent will raise his rates. Sometimes sooner. The agent can afford to be generous because the agent's interest is closely tied in with the child's interest. The more money the talent makes, the more money the agent makes through commissions.

Print models have hourly and day rates. They are guaranteed an hour rate minimum even if they only work five minutes. The rates do vary depending on which market you work. They can fall in a range anywhere from a $40 an hour for a baby to $150 an hour for an experienced model. The average hourly rate is between $50-$75 an hour.

A day rate translates into eight times the hourly rate. There are three basic categories in print modeling where the rates go up according to the exposure the ad gets throughout the country. The three categories are: Point of Purchase (POP), Packaging and Billboards.

Point of Purchase (POP) means that a model's face, likeness or image is at a point where a consumer makes a purchase. For example, if you are shopping at a Disney store, and see a poster of two children showing off their Mickey Mouse watches, their face is at the point where you make a purchase. This is called "point of purchase." The models are on display the entire time the store is open. Garment tags with children's faces on them are point of purchase. It doesn't matter whether you are shopping at a department store, drugstore or fast food franchise — it's called point of purchase advertising if a model's face is displayed at that location.

Packaging refers to a model's photograph, image or likeness on a box or package. Babies and children are commonly seen on diaper boxes, swing set boxes, baby food jars and cereal boxes.

Billboards are the large signs placed along highways and major intersections. Mini-billboards can be found on the side of buses, on the top of cabs and in subway stations, train stations and airports. Any child whose photograph is displayed in this form of advertising is also paid a special rate.

To help you make sense out of the varying pay rates of the trade, here is an easy reference table delineating how the compensation breaks out for these special areas of print. Notice how the model's pay rate escalates according to the amount of location exposure this form of print advertising receives. Again, the rates may be negotiated higher or lower, depending on the market. These are the competitive print rates for Atlanta, Georgia.

SINGLE CITY *refers to advertising which appears in only one city in a state other than the largest city, such as Buffalo, New York; San Diego, California; or Macon, Georgia.*

LARGEST CITY OR STATE *refers to advertising which appears in a city such as Los Angeles, Atlanta or New York City. State refers to an entire state.*

REGION *refers to advertising which appears in large blocks of the country. There are six different regions: Southeast, Southwest, West Coast, South Central, North Central and Northwest.*

NATIONAL *refers to advertising which can appear anywhere in the United States.*

POINT OF PURCHASE (POP)

LOCATION	PACKAGING	BILLBOARD
	Pay Rates	Pay Rates
SINGLE CITY	Day Rate + $100	Actual Time Worked + $100
LARGEST CITY OR STATE	Actual Time Worked	Day Rate + $200+ $200
REGION	Day Rate + $200 Actual Time Worked	Day Rate + Actual Time Worked
NATIONAL	Double Day Rate +$200 + Actual Time Worked	Double Day Rate + Actual Time Worked

POINT OF PURCHASE RATES

Model:
Richard Manus

The following is an earnings example of a real life model — seven-year-old Richard Manus. Richard worked two hours for ARBY'S as a print model. They produced a poster, with his picture on it, that will hang in the ARBY restaurants. This "point of purchase" piece will appear in the Southeast Region. Let's see how much Richard earned.

POINT OF PURCHASE	
FORMULA FOR REGION PAY SCALE:	Day Rate + 200 + Actual Time Worked
Model Name and Hourly Rate:	Richard Manus earns $75.00 an hour.
Day Rate (8 hrs. x $75):	$ 600.00
Add $200 for region Exposure:	+ $ 200.00
Add Actual Time Worked(2 hours x $75.00)	+ $ 150.00
	$ 950.00

Richard Manus earned $950.00 for two hours work.

$ $ $

**POINT OF
PURCHASE
RATES**

Model:
Katy Shuman

This next example is of nine-year-old model Katy Shuman. She worked 1.5 hours for HARDEE'S. They put her face on the HARDEE place mats that are placed on the restaurant's food trays. This "point of purchase" piece will be used NATIONALLY— that is, it can be used by any HARDEE'S in the United States.

POINT OF PURCHASE	
FORMULA FOR NATIONAL PAY SCALE: Double Day Rate +$200 + Actual Time Worked	
Model's Name and Hourly Rate:	Katy Shuman earns $75.00 an hour.
(Double 8 hrs. X $75.00)	$1,200.00
Add $200 for National Exposure:	+ $ 200.00
Add Actual Time Worked(1.5 hrs. x $75.00):	+ $ 112.50
	$ 1,512.50

In addition, HARDEE'S used the same photograph of Katy Shuman to print a "billboard." This means Katy will receive the additional billboard rates. Her billboard rate is $1,312.50. If we add that on top of her point of purchase rates, Katy Shuman earned $ 2,825.00 for 1.5 hours of work.

May 9-10th

gia Bone 1 Day Suite (Fund)

AFTRA/SAG ATLANTA
1627 PEACHTREE STREET, NE - SUITE 210
ATLANTA, GEORGIA 30309 - PHONE (404) 897-1335

TALENT CONTRACT AND STATEMENT OF CHARGES

EEOC CATEGORY (OPTIONAL): _____

№ 11584

THIS EMPLOYMENT IS UNDER : ☐ AFTRA ☑ SAG

☐ SCALE ☐ SCALE + 10% ☐ OVER SCALE @ _____

PENSION AND WELFARE TO BE PAID BY:

EMPLOYER OR REPORTING COMPANY: *Talent Partner*

PRODUCT / PROGRAM: *One Day Sale*

COMMERCIAL I.D. #: *DTV 1010*

ADDRESS: _____

JOB #: _____

PRODUCER: *D. Kolka*

ADDRESS: _____

TOTAL GROSS PAYMENT TO PERFORMER: $ _____

CONTRIBUTIONS: RADIO ___ % $ _____

TV ___ % $ _____

AD AGENCY: *DtP*

OTHER ___ % $ _____

ADDRESS: _____

TOTAL P&W REMITTANCE $ _____

MAKE P&W CHECK PAYABLE TO:
AFTRA P&W OR SAG P&W. SEND TO AFTRA/SAG
WITH PINK COPY.

STUDIO: *Cinema*

CITY AND STATE: *Atlanta, ga.*

DATE FIRST USED (BROADCAST): _____ / DATE FIRST USED (CABLE): _____

REGIONAL USE ONLY - (GA., S.C., N.C., AL., MS.)	NATIONAL USE ONLY	INDUSTRIAL / NON-BROADCAST
☐ RADIO	☐ RADIO - ☐ 13 WEEK ☐ 8 WEEK	☐ O/C ☐ V/O # PROGRAM(S) ___
☐ TV - ☐ O/C ☐ V/O	☑ TV - ☑ O/C ☐ V/O	☐ CATEGORY I OR ☐ CATEGORY II
☐ WITH ATL. + ADD'L UNITS (#___)	☐ DEMO	☐ NARRATOR SPOKESPERSON
☐ WITHOUT ATL. + UNITS (#___)	☐ TAG(S) (#___) *16*	TYPE OF CONTRACT
CYCLE OF USE	☑ WILD SPOT (# *16*) ☐ N.Y. ☐ CHI. ☐ L.A.	☐ DAY PLAYER ☐ 3 DAY ☐ WEEKLY
☐ 3 DAY ☐ 1 WEEK ☐ 4 WEEK	☐ DEALER - ☐ A OR ☐ B	☐ RETAKE/REDO
☐ 13 WEEK ☐ 52 WEEK ☐ DEALER	- ☐ WITH N.Y. OR ☐ WITHOUT N.Y.	☐ AFTRA NON-BROADCAST
	☐ PROGRAM SPOT CLASS: ☐ A ☐ B ☐ C	☐ AFTRA SLIDE FILM
☐ SINGLE MKT. RADIO ☐ HOLDING FEE	☐ HOLDING FEE	☐ SAG INDUSTRIAL FILM
☐ TAG(S) (#___) ☐ REINSTATE	☐ REINSTATE SINGLE MKT.	☐ GENERAL EXTRA
☐ DEMO ☐ CABLE ONLY	☐ CABLE ONLY ☐ RADIO	☐ SPECIAL ABILITY EXTRA
☐ SEASONAL	☐ SEASONAL	☐ SILENT BIT
# OF SPOTS: ___ RADIO ___ TV	# OF SPOTS: ___ RADIO *1* TV	☐ SINGERS - ☐ S/D ☐ GROUP (#___)
TYPE OF PERFORMANCE ☐ ANNOUNCER ☑ ACTOR ☐ SINGER (#___) ☐ DANCER (#___)		
☐ HAND MODEL ☐ EXTRA ☐ MULTI-TRACKING ☐ SWEETENING		

DATE OF EMPLOYMENT: *4/19/89*

HRS. EMPLOYED: (FROM) *2:00m* (TO) *6:30m*

NUMBER OF WARDROBES SUPPLIED _____

	MEALS	FITTING/MAKE-UP	TRAVEL TO	TRAVEL FROM
	FROM : ___	DATE : ___	DATE : ___	DATE : ___
	TO : ___			
	FROM : ___	FROM : ___	HOURS : ___	HOURS : ___
	TO : ___			
		TO : ___	MILES : ___	MILES : ___

NAME *Gia Bone*

S.S. # *251-69-6701*

F.E.I. #

TALENT AGENT

This document constitutes a contract between Employer and performer for the services indicated as well as the appropriate payment for session fees, reuse, replay and residual fees specified in AFTRA/SAG Codes and Contracts. The signing of this report by the Employer shall be deemed an acceptance by the Employer of the pension and welfare provisions of the AFTRA/SAG Codes and Contracts under which the work was performed, and an agreement by the Employer to be bound thereby and by the Pension and Welfare Funds/Plans established thereunder.

Kidding Around by Anne Bone 4/19/89

PERFORMER'S SIGNATURE   DATE

D. Kolka 4/19/89

EMPLOYER'S SIGNATURE   DATE

PERFORMER AUTHORIZES PAYMENT TO BE SENT TO ☐ SELF OR ☑ C/O TALENT AGENT AT:

ADDRESS:

№ 11584 **WHITE - AFTRA/SAG - ATLANTA** **YELLOW - PRODUCER'S COPY** **PINK - P&W FUNDS**

Example of a union contract

TV Commercial Rates

In the great land of TV commercials, we come across a completely new and different way of computing pay rates. These rates of payment are governed, for the most part, by two unions. The names of these unions are AFTRA (American Federation of Television and Radio Artists) and SAG (Screen Actors Guild). The Unions represent people as diverse as Tom Brokart and Meryl Streep. They represent puppeteers, variety actors, news announcers, industrial and feature film actors, TV actors and TV commercial and radio talent. They only represent on-camera (actors) and off-camera (voice-over) talent.

The union's primary function is to negotiate wages and working conditions, enforce contracts and attempt to implement the needs and desires of the Union members. They currently have approximately 94,000 members comprised of children and adults — black and white, Hispanic and Oriental. There are no groups excluded. However, it's not a piece of cake to become a member, and annual dues must be paid for members to remain under union protection.

Not every state falls under union jursdiction. Some states, such as Georgia and Texas, are "right to work" states, which means agents in these states are not required to hire union actors and actresses. However, the payment rates established by the union for talent are basically adhered to by agents located in every part of the country. This means that whether or not it becomes necessary for your child to become a member of the union, he will be paid, in most cases, the same wages as union members.

TV commercial acting is one of the highest paying divisions of the business. Not only is the talent paid for the time he works, but he also receives "residual" payments. These "residuals" are what push the talents wages into the high income brackets.

The initial payment for on-camera talent is a session fee of $366.60. This includes work done within an eight-hour day. So, if your child only worked five hours on one particular day, he would be paid the basic session fee. The residual fees are paid on top of the session fee. They are based on the number of markets the TV spot will run in and how long it will air.

Generally, an advertiser books commercial air time in segments of 13-week cycles. A performer is paid for every 13-weeks a spot will run on television. The exact amount of payment is determined by the number of television market areas it will run in, and the number of units or television households assigned to each market.

UNIONS

❏ **AFTRA** (American Federation of Television and Radio Artists)

❏ **SAG** (Screen Actors Guild)

© Copyright 1989
TALENT PARTNERS.
CHICAGO, ILLINOIS

TALENT PARTNERS

303 East Ohio Street, Chicago, Illinois 606 11

AD AGY/PROD CO.			AGENCY		
CHIAT-DAY 1538					20

COMMERCIAL ID #	ORIGINAL ID #	EDIT VERSION #
NONTO215	NONTO202	

ADVERTISER	PRODUCTS
NISSAN MOTOR CORP	STANZA

TITLE	UNION	DATE 1ST SERVICE	YEAR CODE	CATE-GORY	CAM-ERA	DOUBLING	% OVERSCALE	SESSION INFORMATION
FAMILY PERFORMANCE :30	SAG	8 12 89	88	P	ON	MO SO DBLS		NO OF DAYS WORKED / OVERTIME HRS 1½X 2X

FIRST AIR DATE	FIRST FIXED CYCLE	MAXIMUM PERIOD OF USE	A.F.M. CONTRACT NO(S).	A.F.M. LEADER	A.F.M. DUB DATE	PREMIUM STRAIGHT TIME
10 02 89	8 11 89	5 11 91	LACC3937			

MEDIA	PAYMENT TYPE	USAGE TYPE	USE WKS.	CYCLE DATES FROM TO	PREMIUM OVER TIME
TV	REUSE	TV CLASS A USES 57 THRU 58	13	10 02 89 1 01 90	

MADE FOR CABLE ONLY		CLASS A USE DATES	/ / / / /	/ /	PREMIUM DOUBLE TIME
MADE FOR SPANISH					TRAVEL HOURS / PRIOR FIT HOURS

				/ / / / /	/	INCLUDE

WILD SPOT INITIAL		WILD SPOT UPGRADE TO			CAN TAX	INVOICE NO.	NO. OF SPOTS
MAJOR CITIES / PLUS UNITS	MAJOR CITIES / PLUS UNITS	AMOUNT APPLIED			N	947013	1

COMMENTS

INQUIRIES TO:	EMPLOYER OF RECORD FOR WITHHOLDING AND UNEMPLOYMENT (U.C.) INSURANCE IS:
TALENT PARTNERS 818-955-5000	TALENT PARTNERS

EMPLOYEE NAME	CHECK NUMBER	DEPT.	UNION	UNION LOCAL	STATE CODE	AGENT CODE	PAY ENDING MO. DAY YR.
JENNIFER N. WALKER	08223190	00	20		GA	4248	11 24 89

SOCIAL SECURITY NO.	FEDERAL I.D. NO.	CORPORATION FSO:	STATE U.C. #
252 47 2640			GA-476060-18

GROSS EARNINGS	MISC. PAYMENTS	REIMBURS. EXP.	MONIES DUE TP THIS PAY	TAXABLE EARNINGS THIS PAY	TOTAL DEDUCTIONS	TAX LIENS/ GARNISHMENTS	AMOUNT OF CHECK
9330				9330	1232		8098

FED W/H TAX	FICA	STATE TAX	SUI	LOCAL TAX	CANADIAN TAX	MISC. DED.	STATE DISABILITY	MPTRF	PERMANENT CHARITIES
505	701	GA: 026							

YEAR TO DATE TOTALS: GROSS EARNINGS	MISC. PAYMENTS	REIMBURSEMENT EXP.	FED W/H TAX	FICA	STATE TAX	LOCAL TAX	CANADIAN TAX
1633445	000	1500	239621	122672	66659	000	000

Example of a residual check

The check made out to your child will be quite large if the commercial runs in highly populated cities. And, the checks will keep coming if the commercial runs for an extended period of time.

Say a commercial contracted to air for nine months. That means the TV spot will run for three 13-week cycles. Your child will be paid three different times — once for every 13-week cycle. The average check for an individual commercial talent, per 13-week cycle, is currently between $1,500 and $2,000. If the commercial ran for nine months, a child could make around $6,000 for a commercial he spent one day in the studio working on.

Since "print model" rates are not governed by union guidelines, they are more negotiable and tend to fluctuate from market to market. There are standards, though, to which most legitimate agencies strongly adhere. But, agents are given the opportunity and flexibility to negotiate with clients, up or down, depending on what the client's budget can handle. On the other hand, the actors in the business, young and old alike, are held within a boundary or structure of pay scales, strict contracts and loads of paperwork.

You should have a better feel now for the "dollars and sense" of the kind of money your child can make, as well as the inner workings of how where and who he will make more money in one area over another.

Your agent's power in negotiating contracts and rates on behalf of your child is an important attribute. But, remember, you and the agent are sailing the same ship. Your child's welfare, both personally and professionally, has to be the agent's primary concern.

Real life model, 11-year old Jennifer Walker, made over $16,000 in two months for only six hours' work. Although Jennifer's cast is an unusually profitable one, it does show the inherent potential for the young professional child talent.

CHAPTER 7

THE VOICE OF SHOW BIZ KIDS

"Allow children to be happy in their own way;
for what better way will they ever find."
— Dr. Samuel Johnson

Portfolio Sampling	**Total Credits**
COCA-COLA	*57 Print Jobs*
IBM	*10 TV Commercials*
J.C. PENNEY	*2 Industrials*
BLUE CROSS / BLUE SHIELD	*3 Fashion Shows*
UPTON'S	
TODAY'S LIVING HEALTH Magazine	
CENTRUST BANK	

"I think show business is a lot of fun. My doctor thought that at the age of three I was very cute, and I had such a great personality that my parents ought to get me in movies."

After the doctor made these comments, Kevin's parents started to investigate and made a few calls to the model and talent agencies. Kevin's first job was with Gayfers in Alabama.

"It was a weird feeling, I was excited, and it happened to snow that day. We were a little leery about traveling in the snow. But at the commercial I had to pretend to be asleep. And that was fun and exciting. I do more auditions and print work. I have never been in the movies or done a play as of yet, but I have done ten TV commercials.

"I took some speaking and acting classes at the local theater. They charged about $200 for six to eight weeks for one-hour classes. It was worth the money because this school taught me how to audition correctly. It also taught me not to be shy in front of the camera. I just pretend I am doing it in front of my mom and dad.

"I enjoy acting in TV commercials because there is more action in TV commercials. The longest I have been on a set was about eight hours. The shortest time was about ten minutes. I had the most fun in a commercial where we had film producers coming from Los Angeles. They sat in director's chairs. There were several mobile trailers, and they did my makeup in one and I dressed in another. It was just real big, very Hollywood.

"The hardest job I had was a Coca-Cola commercial because it was freezing outside, and we had to work for a couple of hours. Dad was in the commercial with me. I had to chew on cold ice so that I would breathe out cold air, and I couldn't get the smoke effect coming out my mouth.

"Mostly my work is pretty easy. I enjoy it. I did have to give up my baseball practice. I have a chance to make up my work in school. My friends are very supportive, and they're not jealous or anything. My brothers and sisters are very supportive, but my grandmother is my biggest fan.

"My advice for other kids who want to get into the business is that it is really fun, and it is exciting to go on auditions. 'Cause sometimes you are going to go on a national TV commercial. It is really an experience, and great to see yourself on TV. When I get a paycheck my parents first put it in the bank and save it for college.

"I want to stay working as an actor as long as I can. But when I grow up, I'd like to be a lawyer or an undercover policeman."

Joanna Hayes
Age: 11
Years in Business: 5

Portfolio Sampling
"Annie Get Your Gun"
LEAD ROLE OF ANNIE
"Sound of Music"
SUNNYLAND
CHANNEL 11
MACY'S
UPTON'S
BULLOCK'S

Total Credits
9 Plays
13 TV Commercials
30 Print Ads

"I started in the business when I was about six, so I have been in the business for five years. I do mostly theater acting, and I do some commercials and a little bit of print. Theater is my favorite. The feeling I get when I come out in front of a lot of people is a little nervous at first, and then when you get out there, it all becomes natural. At the end, it is really great because all of these people are standing up applauding for you.

"I get into the character I am playing, but I don't really take her home with me. When I was smaller, my family would play the other parts. This enabled me to practice better. I think I like theater better than commercials. Even though they both have animation, you can't be as big in commercials. But on stage, you have to be really big. In commercials, you just animate and you are normal.

"You have to learn to take rejection in this business. But it really depends on if I really want the part real bad. I used to be really into Annie the orphan at the age of three, and I wanted to go see the play at the local theater. Then I realized that I wanted to be her, I wanted to sing and act. At the age of five, I went out to try for the part of Molly in the play 'Annie,' but I didn't get it. This was very disappointing to me. My mom gets more disappointed than I do."

A few years later, Joanne had the opportunity to audition for the leading part in "Annie Get Your Gun." This time her efforts paid off.

"The most fun thing I have ever done in this business was when I played the part of "Annie." I did 71 shows in all. My mom would ask me how I could stand getting up there and doing a great job 71 times. It is important to me how my performance affects an audience. I like to see their reaction. It was a different audience every night. It gave me the energy."

Joanna has an unusually busy work week for a girl the age of eleven. Her schedule, full of activity, doesn't leave much time for socializing.

"The hardest thing for me is giving up my social life. When I was doing my play, I would go to bed at 2:30 a.m. and have to wake up at 6:00 a.m. Sometimes that would leave me with only having two hours of sleep every night."

"I think you can never get enough training. Each time I take a workshop I feel like I am learning more. It helps you at being more professional and you have a better chance of getting more auditions because of what you have learned."

Joanna has earned several thousands of dollars during her five-year career. Her parents place the money she earns in a savings account in her name. However, Joanna is paying the expenses of a private school she has chosen to attend.

"When I am sixteen I'd like to buy a cool sports car. Then I will save the rest for college. I want to major in drama. I would like to be an actress when I grow up. If I don't make it in that, then I want to be some kind of designer. If not that, I would like to be a makeup artist and hairdresser.

"The best thing I have gotten as an actor is that I have become more mature and responsible. You have to give up a lot of things, time mostly. It is harder than you think it is, once you get into it. You have to be strong to be in it. You can't just give up. You have to go for it — because that is what I did."

Joanna's Normal Weekly Schedule

Monday
This is what my week is like. First I go to school and then I go to voice. The voice is for my singing. I am an actor, dancer and singer. Then I eat, and afterwards I go to ballet. Then I go to tap, and all these classes are on Monday. I get up in the morning at 6:30 or 7:00 a.m. I get home in the evening at 9:00 p.m. When I get home I do my homework, and then I get to bed around 10:00 p.m. I am on the president's list at school. I have to keep my grades up.

Tuesday
I go to school, then I have jazz for two hours. Then I come home and do my homework. I get home about 8:00 p.m. When I was in "Annie Get Your Gun," Monday was an off day in the theater, but I worked Tuesday through Sunday. On Saturday and Sunday I would have two shows, a matinée and a night show.

Wednesday
I go to ballet class for two hours after school. I get home at 8:00 p.m.

Thursday
I go to school, and then I have ballet and jazz classes for three hours. I get home at 9:00 pm.

Friday
I have a tour show with a group of kids that we audition every year, and put a show on at local play-houses.

On the weekends I sometimes have a workshop.

91

Katy Schuman
Age: 8
Years in Business: 4

Portfolio Sampling	Total Credits
GAYFERS	100 Print Jobs
HARDEE'S	4 TV Commercials
MACY'S	
RICH'S	
SIX FLAGS OVER GEORGIA	
J. C. PENNEY	

"I have been a model for about four years, which is most of my life. I have done commercials and magazine advertising. I enjoy being in TV commercials the best. I like being on TV.

"Acting and modeling is simple. It is simple to do the motions. It is both hard and simple to read a script. It could be hard to remember the lines, but it could be simple to read them. I've never forgotten my lines.

"The hardest thing I did was working on the TV series '911.' I had to pretend I stabbed somebody and it was kind of hard to get into. Then there was a movie audition I went on. I really worked hard learning lots of lines for it. But another girl matched more of what they wanted.

"I am in the third grade. I was on the honor roll last year. My other activities are piano and dancing. I am in a group called the 'Little Generals' and they toured the country. I have appeared on the Grand Ole Opry and at the White House. I danced for Mrs. Nancy Reagan. I have done about four commercials, and about 100 print jobs. I liked when I did the Disney channel commercial audition, and I got to jump rope."

Katy's advice for other little girls in modeling is to "just smile a lot, and if you are in a commercial — remember your lines."

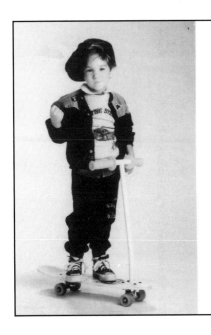

Portfolio Sampling

Hardee's
Macy's
Channel 2
Rich's
Atlanta Journal Constitution
Mansour's
Broadway Southwest
3 Yrs. Dancing with
    "Little Generals Cloggers"

Total Credits

50 Print Jobs
6 TV Commercials

Dan Schuman
Age: 7
Years in Business: 3

"I have done about 50 or 60 clothing ads, and I have done about four commercials. I like commercials the best. I sometimes have trouble remembering my lines.

"I am in the second grade, and I make good grades. When I grow up I want to be in the navy, and I want to fly planes.

"The most fun I had was doing the Tylenol commercial. I got to play with puppies. If I had a choice of kissing a dog or a girl, I would kiss a dog."

Nate Schuman
Age: 11 years old
Years in Business: 2

Portfolio Sampling
BELK'S
RICH'S
HART'S
WHITEWATER
WALDEN KIDS
ZIGLER MEATS
CHANNEL 11
5 YEARS DANCING WITH
    "LITTLE GENERAL CLOGGERS"

Total Credits
25 Print Jobs
6 TV Commercials

"The worst part of the business I guess is that sometimes I have to leave school to do a job. But I get to meet nice friends modeling and improve on my social skills. I used to be real shy.

"I would encourage a kid to get into the business because it is a lot of fun. But I wouldn't encourage them if they had a lot of things or activities that they are already involved in."

"I'm hoping to be a marine biologist when I grow up. I work in mostly print and voice-overs. A print jobs is real quick. They take your picture at the audition, and they call you if you get it. You come back to take pictures and they print them out and you are gone.

"Commercials are the most fun because I get to see myself on the monitor and see how I look. For a commercial it takes maybe about five hours if you do not get it just right. I did an 'Il Alive' commercial where I didn't have a speaking part. I had to eat nine popsicles. It took me from eight in the morning until nine at night.

"I did another commercial for Zigler's hot dogs. It took about six hours and they had me eating hot dogs and bologna. I do not like bologna. I just ignored the taste of it, but I enjoyed it because it paid well.

"I had the most fun doing a commercial for White Water, a water amusement park, because I got to go on the rides during the commercial, and I also got a free pass.

Trista Barfield
Age: 14 years old
Years in Business: 3

Portfolio Sampling
Macy's
UPTON'S
KIDS STORE

Total Credits
100 Print Jobs
10 TV Commercials

"I do more fashion print modeling than anything else. I love clothes. The first year I started modeling professionally I really worked a lot, sometimes three or four days a week. But now, I am a size 14 or a 1 or 2 junior and it is slowing down now. I am at a weird age, and not able to wear the popular sample size 10 anymore. I still practice at home and take a few classes.

"I've never really considered any of the jobs I've done hard. I like it a lot and it is really easy. I guess the interviews are the hardest because you really want to impress them but you are nervous. It comes natural to me. If you don't feel comfortable in front of the camera, it is going to be pretty hard to do this kind of stuff because you really have to be energetic and open with a camera. Sit up straight and all of that. And you have to feel comfortable with all the new people that you meet.

"My mother allows me to do this because I want to. I don't think people should force their child to do anything they don't want to do. It is really sad to see the kids have to do it because they get nervous, they get sick and throw up all over the place. There was a little girl the other day who was on an interview and threw up everywhere.

"For me, it's a good feeling to be told I am good and that I am special. I like the attention and the money. I want to be rich and famous either as a model, fashion designer or maybe an interior decorator. I like to decorate a lot."

Graham Seagraves
Age: 12 years old
Years in Business:
*   4 months*

Portfolio Sampling
RICH'S
MACY'S
UPTON'S
BELK'S
HECK'S
HART'S

Total Credits
20 Print Ads

Graham's parents did not have to go through the traditional method of submitting photographs to a talent agent. He is one of those unusual kids whose discovery was not preplanned by either parent or agent. Another situation unique to Graham is that his father assists him on his modeling assignments. His father takes the calls for his bookings and drives him around to his print "go-sees" and print shoots.

Graham talked excitedly about that special winter's day that changed his life. "My mother had a trade booth at a 'baby expo' and I was there at the Civic Center helping her. We were taking a break from our booth, and walked up to a modeling booth set up for baby models and some children.

"My mother and I walked up and she saw this little sheet. It had some questions on it, and when we read the questions, my mother just thought it might be a good idea to start modeling. It sounded like fun to me. The agent there said it was a very good idea. That was on a Sunday. I went on my first modeling assignment that Tuesday.

"The first time I modeled the back of my pants was all cut up. I had to have tape around them because my underpants were showing from the back. I felt a little strange anyway, and there were women around so that made me feel even more strange.

"I had a lot of fun the time I worked with a donkey. We were on Arabian Mountain and I modeled with Fred the donkey — that was an experience. I was a little frightened of him because he was kind of big. After that day I can remember saying, 'Gosh, I hope I don't have to smile again for two days.'

"I guess the worst part is the jealousy of some friends. My brother and sister have been really supportive. At first they thought my modeling was ridiculous. But they are now real supportive. When people come to our home, the first thing they bring out is my portfolio and let them look through it.

"My advice for other kids is to fix your hair a lot like I did. I looked at the ads, and I practiced as if it were me. I've learned in the short time I've been doing this to feel more comfortable around people — now more than ever before."

CHAPTER 8

FAMILY TIES AND TALES

"Perhaps a child who is fussed over gets a feeling of destiny; he thinks he is in the world for something important and it gives him drive and confidence."

— Dr. Benjamin Spock

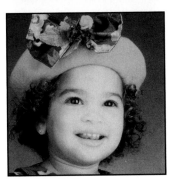

There is no question that the talent industry provides an excellent learning experience for children who enjoy the work. The parent's role in making that learning experience healthy and constructive for the child is fundamental. For the parents are the foundation, the rock on which the child stands as he becomes part of an adult profession. Without the parent or guardian lending constant support and balance, the child cannot go very far in show biz.

Commitment, patience and flexibility are key to both parent and child. It's a family affair, and your influence can make the child's experience as a model or talent fun and stimulating or a complete disaster.

The Sting of Rejection

How to handle the disappointment of not being chosen for a part in a commercial, or as the model for an ad is one of the most serious issues for children and parents in the business. As a parent you have the ability to transform the agony of defeat and disappointment into an attitude of love and support. Jean Tootle, father of eight-year-old model Ben Tootle, talks candidly about how the child and family are affected.

"The biggest disappointment that Ben had was regarding a particular commercial he had auditioned for. He had three call backs for this one national commercial. He was six years old at the time. Because of the number of call backs, we all really, really wanted him to get the job. Then they had gotten it down to two kids of which Ben was one. At the very last minute they called up and said, 'Hey thanks so much, but we decided to use a little girl.' We were very disappointed and unfortunately we projected that to Ben. He began to feel bad because WE were disappointed. And that was a very horrible lesson for us to learn. From that we have learned to approach this business entirely differently. We look at auditions as being fun. We do not worry about call backs — we don't even worry about jobs."

Danny, the father of ten-year-old show biz kid, Kevin Moody, has also had to deal with the pressures of disappointment. "You have to be ready to accept that it is not necessarily anything that you have done to lose that job. It is just a certain look that a producer is looking for. We do not express our disappointment in front of him. They say it can take 19 or 20 different auditions before you can get a good part in a TV commercial. We have found that to be true."

Kevin's mother, Brenda, agreed with her husband wholeheartedly. "Do not ever show the disappointment that you feel to your child. Keep it to yourself. Never get irritated, speak or act rudely when your child does not get a booking or an audition."

Lynn Hayes, mother of eleven-year-old actress, Joanna, admitted she learned the hard way. "There is so much rejection in the business. Sometimes parents take it hard and say 'Wait a minute, did I not fix her hair right?' I took it personally because I try hard to please. They don't care about your child per se; they are trying to fill a spot. They are just looking for a product. Sometimes it hurts. If you can't handle it, you will put it off on your child and that will ruin it for them."

Judy Shuman is the mother of three talent kids. She has been in the business for five years, chauffering her children from one audition to another. "Sometimes some of the people that you come in contact with are very friendly, but some are very curt. You are going in to an audition thinking that your child is the one, but you have to maintain some objectivity to realize that it is not your child or his looks they didn't like. It just wasn't the look the client was looking for. That is not always easy. Sometimes you come away thinking, why didn't they select them?

"Recently my daughter Katy and I went on an audition and I would have loved her to have it. She did very well on the audition, and then I watched another girl audition. She was a very cute little girl. She did just fine, too. After she had finished the client said, 'Thank you very much but I'm sorry.' This child broke into tears and said 'I know I did horrible—I didn't jump rope good.' Instead of getting a hug from the mom, the mom said you are right, you should have smiled a little bit more. The look on this child's face was just unbelievable. I thought, if I ever get to that point, I hope somebody stops me and says, 'Hey you are not building self-esteem in your child.'

"The moms can sometimes be very pushy. When they arrive in the studio they immediately seem to be pushing their way along. They want to go in with their child. When I arrive, I consider myself a taxi. My job is to get them there and to get them dressed. Unless I am invited by the client to actually go on the set, I usually do not. Many moms are not that way. I have heard moms say their child does not go in without them. I find it reflects negatively on the children."

The Stage Parent Syndrome

Think about whether your child really wants to do this, or if you are doing it for yourself:

❏ Are you living your dreams through your child?

❏ Do you want to control your child's choices, or do you want them to make their own decisions?

If you take the time to sift through your own feelings first, you will be open to honestly hearing the voice of your child, instead of your own.

Many parents fall into the trap of living their life through the child's career. They take the child's rejection as a personal affront. Overactive egos get the best of them, while the child gets the worst of it. This can be avoided with a little soul searching from the parent before pursuing the career.

The classic "stage parents" are those that push their way through every audition and every shoot as if their lives depended on it. They try to direct everyone, from the talent agent to the photographer. Stage parents are overly critical of the child's performance and compare him to every child they see. At the same time, they can be found bragging about their child and his success to every mother they can find.

Talent agents will refuse to represent a child, no matter how promising he may be, because of an overbearing, overanxious parent. Clients will not work with children more than once when the parent is overly pushy or gets overly involved during a shoot. It takes a special parent to find the balance between being an active player in the child's profession, and taking a back seat while he's performing.

Lynn Hayes got caught in the "stage parent" trap, but quickly realized that she was causing her daughter and her daughter's career more harm than good. In one particular instance, it lost her daughter Joanna a job. "We were called in by our agent to do a voice-over at a radio studio. Normally, at the dance studios, all the mothers are sitting there saying, oh we are going to win on this audition and everybody talks, talks, talks . . . You do it because you want to pump yourself up because you are getting this big ego trip on what your child is doing.

"I just couldn't wait, so I said to the mother next to me, 'Did you get a call for the voice-over?' I also said it to a couple of other mothers in the waiting room. Well, I said it to a mother who is very pushy. She nonchalantly went in and asked the producer if her child could read for the part. Because of this she got in, and that child got the job over Joanna. Only because I opened my big mouth.

"When Joanna heard what happened, she said, 'Mother, keep your mouth shut about my business. Do not brag. I don't even tell my teachers or friends. It is our business, mother. You are not a talent agent.' I was creating competition that didn't exist. Now I drop my kid off and pick my kid up because I get too caught up in it. I've learned that you go to an audition and keep your mouth shut. You may listen, but it's best not to contribute or talk about your child's business. You do have to be careful not to get caught up in it."

Do Y-O-U Have What It Takes?

Since a child cannot possibly run his own show biz career, a parent, relative or someone specially appointed must assist him. The young professional needs someone to completely manage his affairs.

For on-camera appearances, a parent must arrange his youngster's schedule, make sure he is dressed and groomed for his job, provide adequate transportation to the assignment, be exactly on time, wait for him, keep track of incoming money and decide how much to spend and how much to save.

If you can realistically adjust to the following list of demands on time and energy, you should be able to successfully juggle a potentially active show biz kid.

PROMPTNESS: Rushing to make scheduled appointments precisely on time with everything the child will need for the assignment.

FLEXIBILITY: Rearranging other schedules to fit in with the child's professional timetable. Able to make and accept the inevitable last minute changes to prearranged schedules.

PATIENCE: Waiting for hours while your child is busy on camera. Allowing the art director or producer to work with your child.

COMMITMENT: Continuing to help the child balance school with his acting career. Willing to devote a good deal of time to the child's career.

MONEY: Understanding that the child may not recoup the initial outlay of cash invested in the photography to get him started. Realizing that if the child does make money, it would probably serve him best by saving it for his college education.

Well, how do you feel? Jean Tootle, Ben's father, eloquently expressed his feelings. "I always tell parents that they need to understand what they are going to have to give up in terms of time in order to even have an opportunity at working. It takes a lot of commitment from both the parent and the child. This is why my wife works only part-time. So she will have the time to devote to Ben's career. She even runs into problems where she needs to take off from her job.

"As far as the money is concerned, it's not a problem for us. Each of our children has costly activities that they are involved in. We look at it in that perspective, just being another activity. If the particular kid has the ability and the commitment, then we have a commitment to offer our kid the opportunity to be involved in that activity. If the kid wants to do it, and the parents are willing to provide an environment where it is fun for them, then it should work out OK. A kid is not going to work well in a rough, tension-pressured environment. It takes a certain type of family environment to support that over an extended period of time. It is a family affair."

In the Moody family, both parents agreed that patience is a virtue no successful parent can do without. "I feel you should always be polite when you take your child on an audition or an assignment," Brenda stated, "even though they may cause you to run 30 minutes or an hour late. It may be for some reason they couldn't help. You should just always be prepared to be patient because sometimes schedules do get behind. If you are rude and hateful, they will probably never use your child again."

From the father's perspective, patience is described in a slightly different way. "You have to have patience in this work and realize that every child is different. Not all kids are going to have the same job, but in time, if he is qualified, he will get the work. Patience is the key. Work with your child to be polite on the set. I have seen cases on the production set, where the kids would be so out of hand that I would hear the producer say, 'I will never use those kids again.' So it is important they know how to act when they get on the set. It then becomes natural to the child, which it did to our child, Kevin. He enjoys it, and it makes us really encouraged to work with him and to put our time into this."

The Dangling Carrot

For every effort expended, there is usually some type of reward. Most parents talk excitedly about the many ways their child has benefited from working as a professional talent. Besides boosting the child's sense of responsibility, the commercial business expands the little one's awareness of *how* the magic of still photography and motion pictures is created. This, in and of itself, is quite an education.

With three children in the business, Judy Shuman has a real feel for the rewards to be reaped. "The big plusses for my children in this business have been their self-esteem. They have learned an awful lot about themselves. They have learned that they are not always the center of the world. There are other kids in the world, and you don't always get what you want. But that doesn't mean that you are any less of a person for that. You do not get every job. If you do get the job that's good — if you don't that is OK too. They have learned a lot of discipline in following directions. They have learned respect. There are times when you can make noise on the set, and there are times when you have to sit and be quiet."

Jean Tootle felt that his son Ben, had gained, among other things, self-confidence. "Ben has had the opportunity to meet people from all over the world. An opportunity to be a part of extremely exciting activities. A chance to do things that most kids, and very few adults will ever have an opportunity to do. The proudest moment was when Ben did his first job. He had worked so hard to get to that point and it meant so much. If he never worked another day in his life, at least he could look back and say, 'I have done it'."

A Two-Timing Kid and

Eleven-year-old Gia Bone is a fashion model living in Atlanta. But she and her mother Anne spent the summer of '89 in New York working 12-hour days, five days a week. Ford Model and Talent in New York had agreed to represent Gia during her three month summer vacation.

Besides being picture perfect, adorable and warm and friendly, Gia wears the much sought-after sample size of 10. She also just happens to be Ford's only black model on file who wears this ever-popular size.

Occasionally there are parents who are willing and able to offer their child an opportunity to experience the flavor of another city. Anne Bone is one of those parents. Not only does she spend the better part of the school year carting Gia from one booking to another in Atlanta, but she jets her to New York for the summer and makes a two-hour commute into the city from Staten Island.

"In New York we worked five days a week, multiple jobs at least two days out of the week," Anne relayed. "Our day would start about six-thirty because we were living quite a way from Manhattan. We had to take a train from Staten Island, then a ferry and once we arrived in Manhattan we had to take another train.

"Usually during the rush hour it was wall-to-wall people. You could barely walk because it was so crowded. You would have to stand up on the train and the ferry most of the time because it was so crowded. But it was fun and quite an experience. We ended up buying a luggage carrier because we had to carry a bag of shoes and her portfolio and we were jumping from one train to another and doing a lot of walking. We would have lunch between jobs and walk to the assignments whenever we could.

Her Mother

"As the mother of this busy model, I am the chaffeur, the tutor, the hairdresser and the manicurist. I have done her nails at night while she was asleep. I've even rolled Gia's hair while she was sleeping. It is hard, but it's worth it because she seems to like it. As long as she likes it, we will do it. It has paid off in more ways than one. She has made a good deal of money and had a nice personality change. Gia is very professional when she is working. Before this, Gia was very shy. Some people would say she was pretty and she would blush and wouldn't talk. But now she talks and makes friends. On one audition she took her portfolio over to another little girl and asked, 'May I see yours?' and they became friends. It has been very fruitful for Gia — she has really come out.

"The best advice I have for other parents is that in the beginning, make sure that modeling or acting is what the child wants to do. That is important. Also make sure that you have a good agent to represent your child. First of all, check out the kids that are working and find out which agent they are working with. Then see what they ask of you in the beginning, what they think you should do to start out in the business. If right away they start telling you that you have to spend a lot of money before they even see the child, then you should be a little leery. So thoroughly check into it before you start with them.

"For other black mothers or ethnic mothers, I would say test the market first. See what they are looking for. You never know, it may just be your child they want, be it black, green or blue. Go for it!!"

TALENT SHOPTALK

"Know you what it is to be a child?
... it is to be so little that the elves can reach to whisper in your ear,
It is to turn pumpkins into coaches, and mice into horses,
lowness into loftiness, and nothing into everything,
for each child has its fairy godmother in its soul."
— Percy Bysshe Shelley

While most parents think their child is absolutely adorable, it does take more than a precious kid and a willing adult to endure show biz. But, if you're saying, "My kid can do this," and "I can handle the business of his rising stardom," then it's certainly worth your best shot. By now, you have a better understanding of the inherent ups and downs of the commercial world, and are ready to explore the right avenue to turn your dream into a reality.

The avenue begins with securing a good talent agent. You won't be able to pass go until you have taken the best photographs of your child you can, and submitted them to a few agents. Where you live in the country and what agencies you submit the photos to, will have a significant effect on whether your child's profile successfully matches those of the market and the agencies.

Talent Agents Coast to Coast

Each agency has its own set of criteria for kids they select to represent. The following is a sampling of agencies across the nation. The agencies' business and talent are profiled so that you can get a feel for how they operate in the various cities. Some of the finest agencies from Dallas, New York, Chicago, Miami, Los Angeles and Atlanta were selected.

DALLAS, TEXAS

Kim Dawson Talent Agency
1643 Apparel Mart
P.O. Box 585060
Dallas, TX 75258
(214) 638-2414

TALENT AGENT: Anne Kent

Accepts Talent from: Newborns - Teens

Percent of Agency Bookings:

Print: 66%   Union: ✓
Broadcast: 34%   Non-Union: _____
Print Hourly Rate: $50   Multi-List: _____
Print Day Rate: (8 x Hr. rate)   Exclusive: ✓

For Fashion Print Only

Maximum Height (Girl): 5'0"
Maximum Height (Boy): 5'8"

Accepted Commuting Distance: Dallas and Tarrant Counties Only

Specialties: Fashion sizes 3T, 5, 10, 12-14, twin babies,
                      good actors.

SHOPTALK with Kim Dawson's Agency Children's Director, Anne Kent, from Dallas:

Question: *What can children gain from modeling and do you have any special advice for parents?*

Anne: "I feel like modeling is good for children because they can gain a lot of experience working with the public. They can meet a lot of interesting people and there is good money to be made. For many kids, modeling is the only way they will be able to afford to go to college. It also sharpens their interviewing skills for jobs later in life.

"Professionalism can't be stressed enough. Parents should treat their kid's career as their own because they can make it or break it for the child. It's a serious business and parents should approach it in that manner. Many children are frequently subjected to rejection. How well they adapt and accept it depends on how well the parents take it.

"To be a model does not an actor make and vice versa. All kids are not necessarily good at both. To be a good actor does not mean you are photogenic and comfortable in front of a still camera.

"Parents need to be made aware of the fact that kids grow in and out of sizes. This means there will be times when their child may work a lot and other times where they may not work at all."

Question: *If a child has been rejected by an agency, should the parent continue to submit photographs to other agents?*

Anne: "Persistence pays off in this business so you should just keep trying if you have trouble initially being accepted into an agency. Modeling agencies are always looking for talent to bring in, much like stocking a store with merchandise. Due to the large number of applications, the larger agencies can sometimes be more selective, often preferring to 'pick-up' more experienced talent as needed. If you are rejected by a larger agency you might want to try getting in at a smaller one. They may be more interested in breaking in brand new talent.

"The Kim Dawson Agency takes in talent into the agency on an ongoing basis because kids change sizes and abilities and clients' requests are always changing. But, we only take on new kids when we have a need or a particular opening."

Question: *What do you think parents should consider important to the child's career?*

Anne: "There are two key things in my opinion to keep in mind: one, the child has got to want to do this. When they don't and it's the parents' idea, it quickly makes itself known through their performance. Two, it has to be fun for them. If not, sooner or later you will be put in a bad situation."

NEW YORK, NEW YORK

Ford Models, Inc.
Children's Division
344 East 59th Street
New York, New York 10022
(212) 688-8628

TALENT AGENT: Barbara Laga

Accepts Talent From: Six Months - Up

Percent of Agency Bookings:

Print: 80%   Union: ___✓___
Broadcast: 20%   Non-Union: _____
Print Hourly Rate: $75   Multi-List: _____
Print Day Rate: $750-Up   Exclusive: ___✓___

Maximum Height (Girl):   58-1/2"
Maximum Height (Boy):   60"

Accepted Commuting Distance: Within New York
                        Metro Area

Specialities: Fashion and character look, children who can do
                      both print and commercials.

SHOPTALK with Ford's Children's Director, Barbara Laga, from New York:

Question: *Would you agree to work with children from anywhere in the United States?*

Barbara: "If children from out-of-state would like to work with Ford, they would have to commit to come to New York at their own expense and to work with us for at least two to three months. It usually takes weeks to promote a child in the marketplace. If they cannot commit for at least two to three months, the child will not have the opportunity to enjoy the full benefits that the New York market has to offer."

Question: *What do you think is the up and downside of the business for kids, and what are the special traits you look for during the interview?*

Barbara: "The modeling industry is great for the kids because it builds self-confidence, comaraderie and a strong sense of self. The downside is that they often have to make a choice. Sometimes they will have to miss out on other things, such as sports and being with their friends. They need to have a strong balance between the two. I feel the parents need to be the child's monitor to make sure the child enjoys a healthy outlook and attitude. A child needs this to compete in the very hectic business of modeling.

"We look for children who have a natural ability at being themselves and having fun. They should be able to project well into the camera. Spontaneity is a wonderful asset for any child. Basically, we are looking for happy kids that can project themselves.

"I will look at pictures sent to me from anywhere in the country. They do not have to go through another agency, a modeling conference or a modeling school. If they include a SASE, we will respond back to them."

CHICAGO, ILLINOIS

Stewart Talent Agency
212 West Superior
Suite 406
Chicago, IL 60610
(312) 943-3131

TALENT AGENT: Director of Children's Division — Kathi Garner

Accepts Talent From: Newborn to Age 20

Percent of Agency Bookings:

Print: 60%   Union: ✓
Broadcast: 40%   Non-Union: ____
Print Hourly Rate: $60-$120   Multi-List: ✓
Print Day Rate: (8 x Hourly Rate)   Exclusive: ____

Accepted Commuting Distance: Up to a five -hour drive away

Specialties: Stewart Talent is a full-service agency. Modeling,
                        commercial, feature film, industrial film, theater,
                        voice over and runway. Fashion, "real people"
                        and character looks — (Caucasian and all
                        ethnic looks)

SHOPTALK with Stewart's Children's Director, Kathi Garner, from Chicago:

Question: *What have you found to be the biggest benefit for kids in the business?*

Kathi: "Modeling builds self-confidence in a child. Our industry is an avenue for children to encounter many new experiences and to meet many new people. The industry is a wonderful way for children to attain monies for their college education. We recommend for parents to set up a trust fund in which their earnings can be held for college.

"Our industry should be considered a hobby, not the main focus or concentration in their lives. I have a philosophy, it should always be fun for the child. School comes first and the business should be considered a hobby. As an example: I have a daughter who is 15 years old and has been involved with the industry. Her main interest happens to be in sports, yet she still enjoys auditioning and being photographed for special projects.

"It is very important for parents to educate their child or children regarding the business. Especially to communicate what will be expected of them on-the-job."

Question: *Are you accepting new talent?*

Kathi: "We are always looking for 'new faces.' Business is very active in Chicago. We have a large fashion and product print market along with commercial, feature film, industrial film and voice-over for kids.

"We prefer to receive 35mm color snapshots that the parents have taken with their personal and statistical information on the back of the photographs. If the talent currently has a composite they should send that to us. We do not return photographs to the parents. We will contact the parents for an interview if we can be of service to them within two to four weeks after we receive the submission."

MIAMI, FLORIDA

Michele Pommier Models, Inc.
Children's Division
1200 Anastasia Avenue
Executive Center, Suite 100
Coral Gables, FL 33134

TALENT AGENT: Barbara Cominsky

Accepts Talent From: Newborn to 5'4" Tall

Accepted Commuting Distance: Up to 1-1/2 hours drive

Specialties: Kids that can go from fashion to product and commercial print, samples size 5 and 10 for girls, and size 12 for boys, kids that have a unique European look.

SHOPTALK with Pommier's Children's Director, Barbara Cominsky, from Miami:

Question: *What do you think are a few "perks" the modeling business can offer children?*

Barbara: "It is a wonderful experience for the children. They have the opportunity to meet a lot of different people. But it should be fun and enjoyable for them. The parents are the ones who need to concentrate on making it fun for the kids as well as keeping everything in perspective. Good grades in school should be the first priority.

"Modeling is a great way to start a child's college fund. I have two boys who modeled as children. They paid for their own college tuition as well as my daughter's. And, they bought their first automobiles."

Question: *What's the formula for success?*

Barbara: "Being a beautiful child is not the end-all in this business. Kids can't be shy because there is no time on the job for a child to warm-up. I believe people start at childhood being comfortable with themselves, and that self-confidence and feeling secure with oneself is a great part to being a successful model."

LOS ANGELES, CALIFORNIA

Nina Blanchard Talent Agency
Children's Division
7060 Hollywood Boulevard
Los Angeles, CA 90028

OWNER/DIRECTOR: Nina Blanchard

Accepts Talent From: Six to Twelve Yrs. Old

Percent of Agency Bookings

Print: 50%	Union: ✓
Broadcast: 50%	Non-Union: ___
Print Hourly Rate: $100-$150	Multi-List: ___
Print Day Rate: (8 x Hourly Rate)	Exclusive: ✓

Accepted Commuting Distance: Less than a 1-hour drive

Specialties: Fashion, TV commercials, sitcoms and movies

SHOPTALK with Owner, Nina Blanchard, from Los Angeles:

Question: *Why do you only accept children from the age of six years and older?*

Nina: "We have a very large adult division of this agency. Currently we only have about 40 kids in our files. Generally, when I need a child younger than six, I use the children of the adult models I have listed."

Question: *What do you especially look for in children that you choose to represent?*

Nina: "The child has got to be interested in the business — not just the parent. When interviewing a child for the agency, I take the child in another room, away from the parent. We will not sign on 'clingers.' We look for well-adjusted kids whose parents have raised them with self-esteem.

"There was one incident where a child from a whole family of talent kids, went on a print go-see. The stylist made a negative comment to the child in the form of a rejection. The mother proceeded to take all the children out of the business. Many times I have found that rejection hurts the kids so much because of what the parents contribute to it. Essentially, if you can't deal with rejection, don't get in the business at all."

ATLANTA, GEORGIA

Kiddin' Around Models & Talent
482 Armour Circle
Atlanta, GA 30324
(404) 872-8582

OWNER/DIRECTOR: Eva Stancil

Accepts Talent From: Six Months to Teens

Percent of Agency Bookings:

Print: 60%
Broadcast: 40%
Print Hourly Rate: $50-$75
Print Day Rate: (8x Hourly Rate)

Union: ____
Non-Union: ✓
Multi-List: ✓
Exclusive: ____

Accepted Commuting Distance: Up to 1-1/2 hours drive away

Specialties: Kids who wear sample sizes for fashion, the "real people" look, and an unusual, different look

SHOPTALK with Kiddin' Around, Owner/Director, Eva Stancil, from Atlanta:

Question: *What does it mean when a child is called a "natural" in the business?*

Eva: "To call a kid a natural is always a great compliment. Generally, it refers to a child who doesn't get inhibited in front of people or the camera, who instinctively moves well and who follows directions easily. Children who love the camera are sometimes called a 'natural ham.' They can get up and move and be crazy. Many times life is a stage to them."

Question: *Why do you think some children shy away from the camera?*

Eva: "Kids who are very sheltered by the parents from involvement with other people can contribute to shyness. It's often linked to a lack of self-esteem and confidence, and when mom isn't around they go inward, hugging up to themselves. These type of kids usually don't enjoy modeling and acting around groups of people."

Question: *What is your advice for parents who are considering the modeling business for their child?*

Eva: "Children need all the love, caring and support a parent can give them in this business. Many times you find just the opposite. The parents are pressuring their child to do well. They even use the argument 'We have spent all this money on you so don't let us down.' It's much better for children to tell them you love them regardless of their performance. That attitude will help overcome the fear and horror of rejection, and encourage the child to do his best."

Five Smart Tips to Remember

1. Help launch your child's career because he wants you to do it. If he is too young to tell you, you'll know by his warm and open reaction to people he isn't familiar with and the receptive way he responds to the camera.

2. Consider the modeling business only if you can afford it. And, only if you won't be worried about losing your initial investment.

3. Don't succumb to solicitation from newspaper ads or from direct mail pieces wanting models.

4. Always thoroughly investigate anyone who approaches you or your child with an offer of instant success. If it's sound too good to be true, it probably is.

5. Be sure and check the references of any talent agency to which you make application for representation. Don't leap before you have taken the time to think it through.

✧✧✧

THAT'S A WRAP!

You are the director of this shoot. The one where your child breaks into show biz. It's only your call for "ACTION" that can ignite the magic of opportunity for him. The spotlight is on and the camera is rolling for your cue. Who knows — it could be the start of something **BIG!**

INDEX